Tim Maia Racional Vols. 1 & 2

33 1/3 Global

33 1/3 Global, a series related to but independent from **33 1/3**, takes the format of the original series of short, music-based books and brings the focus to music throughout the world. With initial volumes focusing on Japanese, Brazilian, and European music, the series will also include volumes on the popular music of Australia/ Oceania, Africa, the Middle East, and more.

33 1/3 Japan

Series Editor: Noriko Manabe

Spanning a range of artists and genres—from the 1960s rock of Happy End to technopop band Yellow Magic Orchestra, the Shibuya-kei of Cornelius, classic anime series *Cowboy Bebop*, J-Pop/ EDM hybrid Perfume, and vocaloid star Hatsune Miku—**33 1/3 Japan** is a series devoted to in-depth examination of Japanese albums of the twentieth and twenty-first centuries.

Books in the Series

Supercell's *Supercell* featuring Hatsune Miku by Keisuke Yamada
Yoko Kanno's *Cowboy Bebop* Soundtrack by Rose Bridges
Perfume's *GAME* by Patrick St. Michel

33 1/3 Brazil

Series Editor: Jason Stanyek

Covering the genres of samba, tropicália, rock, hip hop, forró, bossa nova, heavy metal and funk, among others, **33 1/3 Brazil** is a series devoted to in-depth examination of the most important Brazilian albums of the twentieth and twenty-first centuries.

Books in the Series

Caetano Veloso's *A Foreign Sound* by Barbara Browning
João Gilberto and Stan Getz's *Getz/Gilberto* by Bryan McCann
Tim Maia's *Tim Maia Racional* Vols. 1 & 2 by Allen Thayer

Tim Maia Racional Vols. 1 & 2

Allen Thayer

Series Editor: Jason Stanyek

BLOOMSBURY ACADEMIC
NEW YORK · LONDON · OXFORD · NEW DELHI · SYDNEY

BLOOMSBURY ACADEMIC
Bloomsbury Publishing Inc
1385 Broadway, New York, NY 10018, USA
50 Bedford Square, London, WC1B 3DP, UK

BLOOMSBURY, BLOOMSBURY ACADEMIC and the Diana logo are trademarks
of Bloomsbury Publishing Plc

First published in the United States of America 2019
Reprinted 2019 (twice)

Library of Congress Cataloging-in-Publication Data
Names: Thayer, Allen, author.
Title: Tim Maia racional vols. 1 & 2 / Allen Thayer.
Description: New York, NY: Bloomsbury Academic, 2019. | Series: 33 1/3
Brazil | Includes bibliographical references and index.
Identifiers: LCCN 2018039854| ISBN 9781501321535 (pbk.: alk. paper) |
ISBN 9781501321528 (hardback: alk. paper)
Subjects: LCSH: Maia, Tim. Tim Maia racional. | Popular
music–Brazil–1971-1980–History and criticism. | Funk
(Music)–Brazil–History and criticism. | Soul music–Brazil–History and criticism. |
Coelho, Manoel Jacinto, 1903-1991. Universo em desencanto.
Classification: LCC ML420.M146 T53 2019 | DDC 782.42164092–dc23 LC record
available at https://lccn.loc.gov/2018039854

ISBN: HB: 978-1-5013-2152-8
PB: 978-1-5013-2153-5
ePDF: 978-1-5013-2154-2
eBook: 978-1-5013-2155-9

Series: 33$\frac{1}{3}$ Brazil

Typeset by Deanta Global Publishing Services, Chennai, India
Printed and bound in Great Britain

To find out more about our authors and books visit www.bloomsbury.com
and sign up for our newsletters.

Dedicated to Paulinho Guitarra, Don Pi, Tibério Gaspar (R.I.P.), Eduardo Araújo, and all of Tim Maia's friends and bandmates who created, alongside Tim, the Brazilian soul sound

Contents

Preface

Tim Maia Racional *is proof that Tim Maia was a genius. He succeeded in making the unmusical musical: taking a dense text devoid of melody and rhythm and creating a timeless work.*

TÁRIK DE SOUZA, BRAZILIAN MUSIC CRITIC[1]

Receiving an unsolicited Facebook message from Brazilian series editor Jason Stanyek inviting me to contribute a volume to the newly launched 33 ⅓ Brazil series ranks at the top of my "pinch me" moments. I'd been a fan of the 33 ⅓ series for years and had devoted passing thoughts to what I might pitch, if I were to pitch the editors an album, but I quickly concluded that my best contribution would be about a Brazilian album, and surely, they wouldn't be interested in something like that . . . . So, you can imagine my surprise.

Tim Maia Racional Vol. 1 and *Tim Maia Racional Vol. 2* immediately stood out as the best choice for a few reasons: (1) their bizarre backstory, (2) the opportunity to correct much of the misinformation about Tim and particularly these recordings, and finally, (3) to explore the important role these recordings play in Tim's recent resurgence in popularity in Brazil and the even more recent discovery outside of Brazil. But really everyone just wants to know why Tim Maia joined the Rational Culture[2] movement, an esoteric and insular community that gained popularity in Brazil during the late 1960s through the 1970s, led by the towering, charismatic, former Afro-Brazilian religious medium Manoel Jacintho Coelho, popularly known as "Seu Manoel"[3] (or Mr. Manoel). Rational Culture, which still exists primarily in Brazil, professes that humans are exiled on Earth and that in order to return to our home planet, Rational Superior, and our Rational ancestors, all one needs to do is read and re-read the thousand volumes of the book *Universe in Disenchantment* and follow its teachings and you will become "demagnetized" and closer to "rational immunization." Tim not only dove head first into this worldview, he also recorded and self-released two albums (and another nearly complete) of some of the best soul and funk music found anywhere with likely the most bizarre lyrics in any language.

The only way to really understand Tim's connection to the Rational Culture community is to look into his personal life, his motivations, his aspirations, his genius, and his failings. Tim—then in his early thirties—was getting older and attempting to start a family, coming to grips with his addictions, and yearning for validation that remained just out of reach. Tim lived his life in the public, incapable of and uninterested in censoring himself, often compounding his problems by making the personal impact the professional. While I can't exactly imagine joining a group with beliefs as extreme as Rational Culture, I've spent the past couple years trying to understand where Tim's head was at, to make sense of his rationale for joining this extreme lifestyle, to understand how Rational Culture influenced the music he recorded and released during this time, and ultimately, to understand why he left.

In January 2013 I was immortalized in the esteemed bastion of cosmopolitan culture, *The New Yorker*, as a "music writer and Maia superfan"[4] and while I don't balk at that handle, my relationship with Tim Maia, his music, the musicians he inspired, and his home country well surpasses simple fandom. With a few crucial publications (liner-notes for the Luaka Bop compilation of Tim's music, *Nobody Can Live Forever: The Existential Soul of Tim Maia*, and my feature article on Tim's life and music in *Wax Poetics*[5]) I've become, to my surprise, one of the few so-called experts on his music and life, at least in the English language.

I first heard Tim Maia on a mixtape my British friend Hugh Dellar sent me. This must have been 2001, so Tim had already been gone for three years. The song was "Azul Da Cor Do Mar" (Blue the Color of the Sea) from Tim's first album and while I was already passionate about Brazilian music, Tim Maia took a little while to work his way into my own personal pantheon of musical gods. That song did motivate me to pick up a double CD import collection of his early hits with a hideous cover consisting of an unflattering photo from the 1990s of Tim's pockmarked face against a safety-cone orange backdrop. The songs, particularly "Réu Confesso" (Guilty as Charged), "Compadre" (Friend), "Gostava Tanto de Voce" (I Liked You So Much), and "Over Again," leapt out of my headphones, clearly a missing chapter in the story of global soul music. I imagined an all-star team of diasporic soul and funk icons: James Brown, Stevie Wonder, Bob Marley, Jorge Ben Jor, and Fela Ransome Kuti.

In my mind, Tim's on the team, too. I'm also imagining these faces carved into the side of a mountain . . . "Mt. Funkmore." The melodies and rhythms of soul music were so clearly imbedded in the DNA of these songs sung in Portuguese; I didn't need to understand the lyrics to make this connection. The obvious question in my mind was "why isn't this guy more famous?" I remember reading obscure notes in Portuguese on a bizarre website referring to these mysterious "cult albums" of Tim's. I was curious, but at the time when rare recordings were difficult to hear without acquiring them, it took some years before I ever heard *Tim Maia Racional* Vol. 1 and *Tim Racional* Vol. 2.

While falling in love with his songs and story, I unwittingly converted my fanboy enthusiasm into actual journalism and, in the process, I became part of Tim's dream to make it big in the United States. With this book, I hope to help, in my own small way, to make Tim's dream come true, if only posthumously.

Acknowledgments

Without the lengthy and detailed conversations with the following individuals, this book would be little more than a compilation and translation of two books about Tim's life and dozens of magazine articles in Portuguese: Paulo Ricardo Alves a.k.a. Paulinho Guitarra and Reginaldo Francisco a.k.a. Don Pi. Tibério Gaspar and Eduardo Araújo, in particular, shared details and stories previously unheard, at least by me. Paulinho Guitarra, Tim's trusted guitar player, bandleader, and dear friend, is also responsible for nearly all of the photos in this book. Paulinho joined Tim's band as a teenage guitar whiz, playing first on Tim's second solo album from 1971 and the next seven albums, through 1977. A quiet and passionate artist, Paulinho doesn't look like your stereotypical R&B guitar hero with his diminutive stature (about 5'3"), light and ready smile. His memories are some of the sharpest from this phase and he's kept lots of other mementos and items from that time, such as a live recording of an entire Tim Maia Racional concert (the sound quality is atrocious, sadly) and Super-8 footage (without sound, naturally) of a Tim Maia Rational concert. His memories provided innumerable anecdotes for Nelson Motta's biography about Tim. In addition to performing with his own Very Cool Band, Paulinho's played a similarly essential role in Tim's nephew Ed Motta's bands over the past twenty years. Having played guitar with everyone from Tim Maia to Cassiano to Lincoln Olivetti and Ed Motta, Paulinho Guitarra is a living legend in the world of Brazilian soul music, a Brazilian hybrid of Ernie Isely and Steve Cropper.

Don Pi joined Tim Maia's band as a pianist just before Tim's entry into Rational Culture, witnessing a majority of the episode from a front row seat as Tim's apartment mate, personal assistant, and legal charge (Don Pi was not yet eighteen years old when he joined Tim's band). Reginaldo Francisco received his *nom de guerre*, "Don Pi," from Tim, which means roughly "Lord Piano," shortly after joining Tim's troupe in 1974. Tim cherry-picked Pi, who opened for the Brazilian soul godfather, from his high school band following a show in Pi's hometown in late 1973. The Jackson Five were a huge hit at this time and as the bandleader Pi was a dead-ringer for a young Michael, being a teenager himself and with his appropriately voluminous afro, singing, dancing, and playing keyboards. As a straight-laced, teenaged musical prodigy, Pi's memories of joining Tim's troop right as he was going through a major transformation are indispensable to this story. He's also a great storyteller who speaks excellent English despite having never lived in an English-speaking country.

His proximity and access to Tim was unrivaled by anyone except for maybe Paulinho Guitarra. "Paulinho and I were the only guys who Tim taught to forge his signature, so we could go sign for his paychecks," Don Pi confirms. After parting professionally from Tim in the early 1980s, Pi gigged and recorded regularly with some of Brazil's biggest names, including Djavan, Gilberto Gil, Jorge Ben Jor, Caetano Veloso, Cesar Camargo Mariano, and Banda Black Rio. He moved to Köln, Germany, during Brazil's economically tumultuous mid-1980s, earning a good living there playing at a variety of night clubs and jazz gigs around Europe. Like Paulinho Guitarra, Don Pi's name is spoken around Brazil in the same revered tones as Motown's Funk Brothers or legendary Memphis studio session aces that American soul music fans speak of.

Tibério Gaspar played a crucial role in Tim's introduction to Rational Culture, responsible for introducing him to the movement's bible, the book, *Universe in Disenchantment*. But more than that he was one of Tim's oldest friends who, unlike the previous two guys, never worked for Tim and therefore could challenge him without fear of losing a spot in Tim's band. The son of a well-known Brazilian academic and mathematician, Tibério quickly transitioned from a performer to a lyricist during Brazil's turbulent and rapidly evolving music scene of the late 1960s, bringing a sensitivity and nuance to his modern compositions (many in partnership with Antonio Adolfo) while disregarding the old-fashioned mores. A true bohemian, Tibério lived (until his passing in early 2017) on a car-free island in Rio's Guanabara Bay, coming to meet me on a bicycle in Rio's old downtown for our first interview. In his seventies, Tibério, resembling an aged hippie with shoulder-length hair, wispy and sun-bleached, jumping between esoteric and mundane conversation topics, was thrilled to talk about his old friend Tim over a joint and some music. Tibério brings yet another fascinating perspective to Tim's life during this time, speaking of the appeal of Rational Culture as someone personally interested in its teachings and worldview without professional or social pressure from Tim.

Tim's old friend Eduardo Araújo had lots to say about Tim's early years struggling in São Paulo and even though he wasn't present during Tim's Rational Culture years, living at the time in São Paulo, they talked regularly by phone. Eduardo helped Tim at a crucial point in his life and career, in the late 1960s, while Tim was struggling to gain traction within the impenetrable Brazilian recording industry. Throughout Tim's subsequent stardom, he always stayed close and loyal to Eduardo, his early champion, friend, and original Brazilian rocker. A native of Minas Gerais, Eduardo Araújo is a big man with a big personality. Knowing what I know of Tim Maia, it's easy to see why the two would be friends, both having loads of charisma and humor. Araújo maintained a close friendship with Tim, at least until Tim's decline in the 1980s, often talking by phone about life, love, and music. Around the same time, Araújo, the son of a rancher, traded in his progressive, hard-rock style for North American–style country music with great success. According to Araújo, his recently published autobiography, *Pelos Caminhos do Rock—Memorias do Bom* (Along the Road of Rock—Memories of The Good One) (Record, Brazil, 2017), sets the record straight about his old friend, Tim Maia.

The definitive document of Tim's life, to date, is Nelson Motta's biography, *Vale Tudo: O Som e a Fúria de Tim Maia* (Anything Goes: The Sound and Fury of Tim Maia). As a musical industry veteran and Tim's friend for many years, Motta not only was there to witness, and even participate in, many of these stories, but also understands where Tim fit within the established music machinery. Tim's close friend and fellow singer of soul-styled tunes, Fábio co-wrote a book, *Até Parece Foi um Sonho* (It Seemed Like a Dream), about his time with Tim, the same year that Motta released his own book in 2007.

Almir Chediak, who was introduced to Tim by Tibério in the early 1990s, was responsible for Tim's last career comeback with his production and inspiration on Tim's 1991 album *Tim Maia Interpreta Clássicos de Bossa Nova*. In addition to writing numerous books on Brazilian music and the lauded series of M.P.B. Songbooks and companion CDs documenting and celebrating the giants of Brazilian popular music in collections of scores and interviews, Chediak, according to his friends, was working on a biography of his friend Tim Maia when he died suddenly in 2003, a victim of an armed robbery gone wrong. While Motta's book has become the definitive work on Tim Maia, I bring up these other projects in order to acknowledge that there are many versions of Tim's story and, with the addition of Araújo's book in 2017 and this book, the tapestry of Tim Maia narratives is only growing. During one of our long Skype conversations, Don Pi showed me his own unpublished stories of his times with Tim, written by hand in a spiral-bound notebook.

Paulinho and Pi live in relative obscurity despite their tremendous contributions to Brazilian popular music, while Tibério is similarly forgotten, a significant footnote to Antonio Adolfo's continuing story. Eduardo handled the Brazilian music business with the same finesse as the broncos he tamed growing up as a rockin' cowboy from the state of Minas Gerais. Paulinho and Pi, alongside Serginho Trombone, Oberdan Magalhães, Paulinho Trompete #1 (Paulo Roberto de Oliveira), and #2 (Paulinho Martins) Valdecir Nei Machado, Luiz Carlos Batera, Robson Jorge, and Beto Cajueiro, deserve recognition for being the "wrecking crew," the "funk brothers" of the Rio de Janeiro–based Brazilian soul and funk scene and the "souldiers" responsible for a majority of the music and some of the songs on the Rational recordings.

I want to thank Antonio Adolfo, Hyldon de Souza, Marcos Valle, João Donato, Laercio de Freitas, and Thalma de Freitas for taking time to speak with me. Thanks also to Alexandre Kassin, better known as Kassin, for his stories about *Tim Maia Racional* Vol. 3, as well as his encouragement to dig deeper and tell Tim's story as it deserves to be told. Thanks to William Luna Jr. and Arthur Luna for the tour of the old RCA studios and insights in the making of *Tim Maia Racional* Vol. 3

Many thanks to Raphael and Christine from Rational Culture who spent several hours with me over Skype and in person trying to explain and clarify some of the more esoteric and complicated elements of the Rational Culture community and belief system.

A tremendous thank you goes to Sergio Martins for his invite to interview Eduardo Araújo with him and for responding to my countless questions about the most bizarre vocabulary conundrums. A big thank you goes to my new friend and fellow Donato-obsessive, Ronaldo Evangelista for some sleuthing on my behalf. I want to thank my *paulista* (São Paulo native) pals: Pedro Smith, Camila Prado, Lígia Rechenberg, and David Galasse for their friendship, encouragement, and cultural context. To my Rio de Janeiro hosts: Bradley Brooks and Fabiana Fernandez, thanks for the hospitality and friendship. Thanks to my Brazilian and American musician and record digger friends who helped out in many small ways: Rodrigo Teixeira, Bruno Morais, Mauricio Fleury, Edson Carvalho, Rodrigo Gorky, Jonathan Kim, and Tee Cardaci. Thanks to the New York Brazilian mafia: Yale Evelev, Paul Heck, Béco Dranoff, Greg Casseus, and Sean Marquand. Other friends and family not yet covered: Elan Kamesar, Brian Cross, Josh Chaffin, Chris Nakayama, Chris Stamm, and Charlie Thayer.

Thanks to my mom, dad, stepmom Cynthia, and mother-in-law, Fern, for helping out so I could finish this book. Finally, I want to thank my ex-wife, Jamie, for supporting me while I completed this book, and to my sons, Phoenix and Miles, who are simultaneously the cause and cure of my writer's block, for providing me with much needed stress relief and unconditional support.

Introduction

Insatiable Funk

"It's all lies! That motherfucker just robbed me of all my money," a booming voice roared from a corner apartment on Figueiredo Magalhães street in Copacabana, Rio de Janeiro. "It was a summer day, sunshine, 38 degrees [100 degrees Fahrenheit] and blue sky," Don Pi, Tim's roommate and keyboard player, remembers. His roommate and one of Brazil's biggest pop stars (both literally and figuratively) was the one screaming from the window down to the throngs of onlookers beginning to gather below. Everyone knew Tim lived in Copacabana, so when an overweight black man with short cropped hair and a booming voice started yelling from the balcony of a luxury apartment building, everybody knew that it was Tim Maia, "with a whiskey in his hand, screaming down to the stopped traffic below." Stepping back from the window for just a moment to get a fresh joint, he's back at the window, even louder than before: "Let me tell you, this motherfucker just robbed my money, robbed my equipment, my woman left me and here I'm going to smoke my joint, and fuck Seu Manoel Jacintho Coelho!" As if correcting the historical record might make this scene seem less crazy, Don Pi feels the need to add that "the only thing that is not true is that people say that he was naked in the window. This was not true. He was just not wearing a shirt."

Figure 1 *Tim Maia appears on Mauro Montalvão's TV Tupi show on September 7, 1975. Accompanied by dozens of Rational Culture followers. Photo courtesy of Paulinho Guitarra.*

The date was September 25, 1975, according to Tim Maia's biographer, Nelson Motta. Just a year earlier, in 1974, Tim Maia, one of the biggest pop stars in Brazil, calmly tore up his contract with international record company RCA Victor for an unprecedented double album of Brazilian soul and funk that was close to completion. He then re-recorded all of the lyrics to promote Rational Culture, a Scientology-like cult founded in Brazil espousing the belief that humans are not from planet Earth and that in order to return to the home planet, one must become "rationally immunized," a process consisting principally of reading and re-reading the thousand books in the *Universo Em Desencanto* (Universe in Disenchantment) series. Tim Maia's existential detour was unprecedented. Historically, famous musicians have taken spiritual flights of fancy: Cat Stevens converted to Islam well after he was hitting the charts; Bob Dylan was briefly a born-again Christian during an artistic dip in the late 1970s; the Beatles' foray into Eastern spirituality came at the end of their run and only added to their counterculture credibility; Sly and the Family Stone bassist and solo star, Larry Graham, became a born-again Jehovah's Witness, and decades later helped convert Prince, but nothing compares to the metaphysical doo-doo Tim Maia fell in at the height of his fame.

Tim Maia was never satisfied. Brazil's number one soul brother had a voracious appetite for both carnal and philosophical indulgences. Among his dozens of hit songs, and others that should've been, you'll find impassioned odes to chocolate, women, mortality, and his hometown Rio de Janeiro. Tim's remembered by the Brazilian public as a fat, arrogant, hilarious, overindulgent, and yet beloved man-child who died too soon. During the latter half of his nearly thirty-year recording career, he became just as famous for the headlines he inspired ("You didn't go to Tim Maia's show? Neither did he"[1]) as his wildly popular remakes of his classic tunes. Tim's body of work is mostly unknown outside of Brazil, though this situation is improving. Almost two decades since his sudden passing at the age of fifty-five, Tim is finally receiving the attention and credit he deserves for his contribution to Brazilian and international soul music. He is remembered not only for his style and considerable chops as a singer, composer, and musician, but also for his sometimes bizarre and always impassioned approach to life, no more so than on his infamous *Tim Maia Racional* recordings.

The eventual recognition of these albums as some of Brazil's best pop music (Volume 1 at #17, placed higher than any other album of his and Volume 2 at #49 in *Rolling Stone Brazil*'s 2007 list of the 100 best Brazilian albums)[2] solidifies Tim's standing as the King of Brazilian soul music, but also makes the case for his inclusion in soul music's diasporic all-star team. Unfortunately, Tim Maia died before his own country, let alone the rest of the world, fully understood and appreciated his legacy in spreading love, peace, and good times as one of soul music's greatest ambassadors. It's all he ever wanted to do: from the first moment Tim heard American rhythm and blues over the radio as a chubby kid in the lower-class northern suburbs of Rio de Janeiro, he knew he was destined to sing this music. Tim's passion was singular, and despite innumerable setbacks and rejections, he always continued to write, record, and entertain, up until the very end. He passed away in 1998 at the age of fifty-five, a week after collapsing onstage in front of a live audience at the Niterói municipal theater, just across Guanabara Bay from Rio de Janeiro.

Beyond Bossa Nova

I do not believe that Brazilian music is going to be the next big thing. I only think that it will become an essential part of the record collection of any connoisseur, and slowly and surely its influence will infiltrate the rest.

BEN RATLIFF, "THE PRIMER: TROPICÁLIA AND BEYOND"[3]

Not only did Tim Maia record these two albums and introduce Rational Culture to people in Brazil and beyond, he's also chiefly responsible for bringing the sounds, styles, and cultural politics of soul and funk music to Brazil. Brazil's racial diversity combined with its long tradition (as in the United States) of popular music that fused European and African traditions nearly guaranteed soul and funk music's successful adoption and merger into Brazil's cultural fabric. This is where it probably helps to know a little bit more about Brazilian culture, society, and music.

Brazil is the country most like the United States in the world, based on Western hemisphere/"New World" geography, population (United States is 3rd while Brazil is 5th), landmass (United States is 4th, Brazil is 5th), and ethnic and racial diversity (hard to find numbers for this, but if you've been to Los Angeles, New York City, São Paulo, or Rio de Janeiro, it's clear). Its bounty of recorded music is deep and diverse, and the country has given the world innumerable popular rhythms and musical styles from the samba to bossa nova to the many northeastern dance styles like *forró* or *lambada*. Not surprisingly, Brazil is said to be the origin of more unique percussion instruments than any other country on Earth. Despite its riches, common knowledge about Brazilian music among listeners outside of Brazil, can likely be summed up by the following list:

1   Carmen Miranda, an advocate of "the Latin American way" and the one with the fruity turban

2   "The Girl From Ipanema" as performed by Stan Getz and João Gilberto with vocal assistance from João's then-wife Astrud Gilberto

3   "Mas Que Nada" as performed by Sergio Mendes & Brazil '66

4   Os Mutantes, Brazilian psych-rock darlings, a cult favorite of the late, great Kurt Cobain

5   Caetano Veloso, who's Brazilian, from that scene in Pedro Almodóvar's *Talk To Her* where he sings "La Paloma" in Spanish

6   Carnaval, which is Brazil's version of Mardi Gras, makes New Orleans' legendary festival look like a suburban block party

7   Samba, a dance and a rhythm with lots of percussion and hip gyrating

8   Lambada, a dance and rhythm where partners dance in extremely close proximity

9   Capoeira, a Brazilian martial art that kinda looks like break dancing

10   Sepultura, a Brazilian heavy metal band.

What you might not know is that the Brazilian music universe contains nearly every style or sound of music you can find in the United States, just sung in Portuguese and probably with some percussive additives. I thought, surely one exception to this must be North American–style country music, but in the process of researching Tim's life, one of his old friends and someone interviewed extensively in this book, Eduardo Araújo, proved me wrong, as he's been playing straight-up American-style country music in Brazil quite successfully for the past few decades.

Tim famously described himself as, "black, fat and rude, formed in cuckoldry, heartbreak and hair loss,"[4] made his breakthrough in 1970 as Brazilian popular music approached a high-water mark of creativity and popularity. Export-ready artists like Elis Regina, Chico Buarque, and Milton Nascimento delivered top-shelf jazz-inflected torch songs, while tropicalists Caetano Veloso, Gilberto

Gil, and Os Mutantes entertained the college set with avant-garde fuzz poetry. Enter Tim Maia with a cannonball into the pool, knocking Elis Regina off her air mattress and drenching a lounging Caetano in his Speedos. Even samba-soul king Jorge Ben Jor had to pause mid-strum to wipe down his guitar. It was the only dive Tim knew. Before Tim Maia, there was no shortage of Afro-Brazilian musicians, singers, or composers, but they were almost always typecast as happy-go-lucky samba singers, and few had any artistic control over their own careers. With all due respect to the famous Brazilian cultural cannibals (Caetano Veloso, Gilberto Gil, Tom Zé, and Os Mutantes), who dominated the Tropicália scene in the late 1960s, Tim Maia was also in the business of *antropofagia* or "cultural cannibalism."[5] The only difference is that Tim cannibalized black pop music, a.k.a. soul, from the United States instead of Anglo-psych à la the Beatles. In the process he birthed a new genre: Brazilian soul music, that went on to dominate the country's pop charts within a decade of its introduction.

Few popular music artists appeal to a true cross section of society: rich, poor, white, black, Latino, Asian, casual music listener to professional music critic. If you're being honest and you don't live in a rockist bubble, for Anglophone pop music the list is not so long: James Brown, the Beatles, Stevie Wonder, Michael Jackson, Prince, Bob Marley, and Beyoncé, to keep current. We reserve a special name for this category: Superstars. Now consider that Brazil is known for music as much as anything else, resulting in a parallel universe of demographics, racial diversity, and pop music. This is just one reason why the genre of "world music" is so useless; it is incapable of explaining the complexity of each individual country in the world and their own long musical histories and their own indigenous musical traditions, one-hit wonders, crooners, rockers, iconoclasts, mimics, geniuses, hacks, musical golden eras, and dry spells.

Brazilian, Black, and Proud!

Tim Maia is currently experiencing a resurgence in popularity since his death in 1998 as Brazilians and people around the world rediscover his formidable catalog, impact, and previously overlooked albums, like his Rational albums. Tim's legacy is complicated mostly due to the fact that he faced tremendous resistance from the establishment that didn't like the idea of a large, outspoken, black singer of imported styles getting too much attention.

Tim's career was like Elvis Presley's in that there was the "Young Elvis" and the "Fat Elvis," except with Tim, both the "young" and "fat" Tims were fat. Show business in Brazil, or anywhere else for that matter, is anything but kind to overweight racial minorities. Tim jumped up and down on the sideline for years watching less talented and lighter-skinned friends mangle his songs up the pop charts. When he finally got his chance in 1969 with a single followed by his first album in 1970, he exploded on to the music scene with his blockbuster debut album. Throughout the 1970s and the early 1980s, Tim Maia was one of Brazil's biggest stars; at his peak of popularity, on the cusp of his Rational adventures, he even rivaled his old band mate Roberto Carlos, Brazil's answer to Elvis Presley.

Nearly a decade prior to his breakthrough, Tim Maia spent five years (1959–64) living in New York state, in the small Hudson river town of Tarrytown just forty-five minutes north of New York City, where he learned to speak English idiomatically and he absorbed the R&B that would blossom into soul music a few years later. Tim's initial attempts at introducing soul music to the Brazilian market fell on deaf years. Even though Brazil and the United States share similar demographics and colonial history, Brazilian racism is distinctly different from the North American variety. Prior to the 1970s, average white, urban Brazilians imagined themselves living in a harmonious melting pot of European, African, and indigenous lineage, what the famous Brazilian sociologist Gilberto Freyre called "racial democracy."

Beginning in the late 1960s, the US civil rights movement made its way to Brazil through the worldwide exposure of outspoken black American celebrities, such as James Brown, Muhammad Ali, and Isaac Hayes. Through these international celebrities, some black Brazilians began to revisit how they viewed their role in traditional Brazilian society. Tim Maia was the first black Brazilian entertainer to thoroughly break from the traditional roles, namely samba, as he introduced soul music with its modern fashions, unapologetic grooves, and outspoken cultural stances to Brazilians of all colors.

"It was a rupture with the past, a way of putting the question of Black and white on new terms," the record executive who signed Tim, André Midani, says. "The samba performers from before had stayed in the kitchen, but Tim and the rest refused to do that and came into the living room."[6] Tim wasn't the first Brazilian singer to attempt to sing R&B music, but he was the first who successfully and commercially channeled the emotional intensity of the soul style while schooling the Brazilian session musicians on the new style's sonic nuances and feel. While Wilson Simonal, Eduardo Araújo, and Jorge Ben Jor merely experimented with stylistic elements of soul, Tim's dedication to the nascent style helped build a movement that would flourish throughout the 1970s and eventually inspire such genres as *baile funk* (electro hip-hop, sonically like Miami Bass) and Brazilian hip-hop in the 1980s.

The overwhelming success of Tim's first albums announced a new style of black Brazilian singer, one that could tackle a James Brown tune with confidence and power, and still deliver a samba or a bossa nova without sacrificing any authenticity. Alongside a wave of civil rights activists, DJ crews, and musicians, Tim Maia helped to define a modern black Brazilian identity that did not accept mass culture's tightly circumscribed role for Afro-Brazilians. Using the English word instead of the Portuguese "negro," the scene, and later, movement, was called "Black Rio."

This shift and Tim's indisputable commercial success signaled a change in the Brazilian pop culture landscape. Maia's enormous popularity in the early 1970s sent a message to the media masters, and nearly overnight just about every record label, and many of the international labels operating in the country, released records trying to cash in on Tim's popular sound and image. Toni Tornado, Tony Bizarro, Robson Jorge, Cassiano, Hyldon, and even Tim's buddy and supplier of stimulants, Almir Ricardi, recorded Brazilian soul and funk albums. The Afro-Brazilian vocal groups—the Golden Boys, Trio Esperança, and Trio Ternura (later Quinteto

Ternura)—who started off as part of the youthful rock fad *Jovem Guarda* (Young Guard) remade themselves in the 1970s like the Temptations, Gladys Knight & The Pips or the Jackson Five. Without Tim Maia there would be no Banda Black Rio, the seminal Brazilian soul and funk band founded in Rio de Janeiro in 1976. Led by Oberdan Magalhães, a regular Tim Maia band member throughout the mid-1970s, and including up to three Tim Maia band alums, Banda Black Rio continued Tim's experiments fusing soul and funk's black and proud swagger with Brazil's rich indigenous and modern musical traditions.

"At any party in Brazil, at some point you have to play Tim Maia, whose songs have become obligatory standards among all social classes," Nelson Motta, Tim's friend and biographer told the *New York Times*. "When you play Tim Maia, the dance floor is guaranteed to fill up."[7] Case in point, at a 2013 concert in New York City at B. B. King's on 42nd Street, Jorge Ben Jor's (one of the few Afro-Brazilian superstars whose fame rivals Tim's) two-plus hour set included only one cover and one tribute song, both in honor of Jorge's old friend, Tim Maia. Apparently, even touring gringos Guns N' Roses knew this little trick, playing a riffadelic cover of Tim's funk bomb "Sossego" to an audience of over 250,000 people at the 2001 Rock In Rio Festival.

If Tim had stopped recording after his first four albums,[8] he would still be remembered as the founding father of Brazilian soul and funk music and a major figure in Brazilian popular music. Thankfully, he didn't stop, but he did change directions and the resulting detour into the esoteric universe of Rational Culture, though only a little more than a year long, resulted in a deluge of bizarre and fantastic music.

An Introduction to *Tim Maia Racional* Vols. 1, 2 (and 3)

Tim Maia Racional Vols. 1, 2, and the posthumous Volume 3, are the ultimate "cult" albums in every sense of the word. These mysterious recordings represent everything a twenty-first-century record collector might want: super-limited, independently produced, pressed and released, and containing world-class music (unknown to most) with a bizarre and intriguing back story. And if you're digging for funky drum breaks or fodder for samples, it's got those aplenty, too. Despite being released by a major Brazilian star at the peak of his popularity, these albums took more than twenty years to be recognized as masterpieces (as the Rosetta Stone) for understanding the birth and evolution of Brazilian soul music. Unless you were in Rio de Janeiro, or a Tim Maia fan at the time of their original release, you probably didn't learn of the existence of these albums until the 1990s or early 2000s, if you lived in Brazil, and maybe a decade later if you lived anywhere else.

Writing these words in 2018, it's hard to imagine how different and more difficult it was unearthing rare recordings like the *Tim Maia Racional* albums just fifteen years earlier, in 2002 when I first heard of them. Imagine, in the early twenty-first century without iTunes or the collective diligence, obsession and bandwidth of countless bloggers, certain out-of-print albums existed only to those who held the original, physical artifacts. Paul Heck helped compile the career-retrospective release about Tim Maia for Luaka Bop records, *World Psychedelic Classics, Volume 4: The Existential Soul of Tim Maia: Nobody Can Live Forever*, released in 2012, and recalls these early days trying to make sense of Tim's catalog from his home in New York City. "Somehow it was elucidated, there was a gap in Tim's eponymous discography around 1974 and 1975, 'what was he doing then?'" Paul caught rumor of these "cult" records. Alexandre Kassin, a Brazilian musician and producer who'd had his records released by Luaka Bop as a member of the "+ Twos" (a rotating trio of a band featuring Kassin, Domenico Lancelotti, and Caetano Veloso's son, Moreno Veloso), "somehow had all this stuff and somehow I got a burn [CD-R] of it and obviously, it was amazingly great and the story was amazing."[9] Thanks to this compilation and more recent official reissues of these songs, Tim Maia's Rational records are no longer only a thing of myth.

Over forty years have passed since Tim Maia's memorable detour into the world of Rational Culture and while he rarely spoke of his experiences from his brief, but intense existential adventure, he left three musical artifacts (the first two released while involved with Rational Culture and the other decades later after his death) that show him at a crucial period in his life and career when his tremendous musical momentum crashed headlong into his own personal, existential anxiety. The bizarre and brilliant albums, *Tim Maia Racional* Vols. 1 and 2 (and 3), were poorly received by the Brazilian public (if they even heard of them at the time of their release) and just a few months after the release of Volume 2, Tim parted ways with Rational Culture, leaving him profoundly embarrassed and nearly destitute. He ordered his band members to throw away any remaining Rational Culture vestiges, from their white T-shirts and painted white instruments to any remaining LPs or singles, significantly contributing to the rarity of these original vinyl releases.

"I have a theory about this phase," said Mauro Lima, director of the 2014 biopic, *Tim Maia*, about Tim's life,[10] in the São Paulo newspaper, *A Folha de São Paulo*: "It was a way for him to police himself, but he just couldn't handle the deprivation."[11] That's one theory. There are many more, some more convincing than others, but none that will ever make "sense" of this bizarre moment in Brazilian pop culture and music. Beyond exploring the background, influences, anecdotes, and sounds of *Tim Maia Racional* Vol. 1 and *Tim Maia Racional* Vol. 2 and the play-by-play of Tim's brief time in Rational Culture, this book will also address four critical questions whose answers will help to explain the significance of Tim Maia's Rational recordings:

1 Besides the bizarre context, what makes these albums unique in Tim Maia's discography?

2 What is Rational Culture and who was the man, the myth, Manoel Jacintho Coelho a.k.a. Seu Manoel?

3 Why were these albums out of print for so long and how and when did they go mainstream?

4 Why are the Rational recordings an ongoing source of controversy for Tim Maia's estate?

The Rational Recordings: Jewels of Tim's Seroma Years

With as much Tim Maia music as I listened to during the course of writing of this book, I started to notice that the albums I kept coming back to, my favorites, all had the same name noted on the back sleeve: "Seroma." Taking the first two letters of Tim's full name, (Se)bastião (Ro)drigues (Ma)ia, Tim gave his publishing company, his production company, his independent record label, his beloved rehearsal studio where most of the music during these years was composed and rehearsed, the same name: "Seroma." The camaraderie between Tim and his bandmates combined with the relaxed setting of the Seroma studios were the essential ingredients to the legendary Rational recordings not to mention the few albums and singles that bookended them. During these few years Tim Maia developed a deep bench of musicians, most of whom would go on to start or join iconic bands. Tim loved having a gang of musicians, a band of his own. His recordings from these years are universally acknowledged as some of his best, with his 1973 and 1976 self-titled albums often singled-out as rival career bests, if not the two Rational albums, all of which were created and rehearsed at Tim's Seroma studio, known fondly as *O Barracão* (the Shed).

What Is Rational Culture?

When this book project came along, one of the first thoughts I had was that I wanted to really explore what Tim Maia got lost in, to really do the research and approach it with fresh eyes, rather than lean on the usual narrative of "Tim Maia joined some crazy cult and made some killer funk records, but don't pay attention to anything about the actual lyrics, because they're bat-shit crazy." Rational Culture might sound bizarre, but it's no more unusual than any number of nonviolent, spiritual communities that popped up in the 1960s and 1970s. Most new religions founded in the United States in the past century emerged after the Second World War with a major concentration springing up in the mid-1960s.[12] However, Rational Culture's roots are older and more likely a by-product of Brazil's rapid transition from a colony to a modern political and economic powerhouse combined with the influx of new cultures and religions than a reaction to the horrors and inhumanity of the two world wars. Rational Culture's origin is particularly fascinating and surely some of this origin story contributed to Tim's seduction.

Rational Revival

Most well-loved albums find their audience upon release, while others, like Tim's Rational recordings, take decades to reach a critical mass of appreciative ears. Tim's first four albums on Polydor, all self-titled and released successively in 1970, 1971, 1972, and 1973, were instant classics chock-full of radio friendly hits, each one successively pushing the boundaries of Brazilian pop music, mashing Brazilian northeastern rhythms like the *baião* and *forró* with rhythm and blues, and claiming artistic territory for black Brazilians who, prior to his breakthrough, were mostly relegated to samba or related "pure" Brazilian styles. Regardless of the albums' critical reception at the time of their release, most Brazilians just never heard Tim's Rational recordings due to their limited distribution and nearly nonexistent radio airplay.

By the mid-1990s a growing audience of mostly younger fans—introduced to these albums via stars like Marisa Monte and Gal Costa, who both covered songs from the albums—sought out CD bootlegs well before the albums' official reissues in the early aughts. Brazilian hip-hop heroes Racionais MCs and Marcelo D2, an alum of the influential Rio de Janeiro hip-hop–rock crew Planet Hemp, dropped clues about Tim Maia and these albums, the former crew famously incorporating the albums' name into their own. Through conversations with younger Tim Maia fans who weren't alive when the albums were originally released, as well as the man who inadvertently started the Tim Maia Rational craze by ripping his vinyl copy to CD-R, we'll explore the reasons for the albums' belated significance and their place in Tim Maia's ascendant legacy.

Setting the Rational Record Straight

Tim Maia Racional Vols. 1 and 2 represent a turning point in Tim's life and musical career, one that cannot be fully understood without looking back to the beginning of his life with some help from his old friends, like Eduardo Araújo and the books written about Tim's life by Nelson Motta and Fábio. While it's nearly impossible to say with 100 percent certainty that the version I'm putting forth with this book is the definitive truth, it is an honest attempt to address some of the mistruths that have plagued Tim's legacy since his passing. In particular, this book attempts to challenge the 2014 film, *Tim Maia*, and its cheap and overwhelmingly negative portrayal of Tim that focused on his pratfalls instead of his tremendous talents and world-class humor. The film as well as the earlier Broadway-style theater version of his story were productions based primarily on Nelson Motta's book, with the film, more so, taking bold and unnecessary liberties with Tim's story. While Nelson Motta's book is considered the definitive version of Tim's story in print, it's not without its faults and sloppy research. "For the family, it was a big surprise," Tim's nephew Ed Motta says referring to Nelson's decision to write a book about Tim, "because they got into a terrible fight years before Tim Maia died, because of a gig or something." For better or worse, Nelson's book is the story most Brazilians know of Tim's life and it's lovingly told and mostly true, "about 90% true," Tibério Gaspar, an old friend of Tim's, estimates.[13]

1 Tim Maia Irrational, 1942–73

The eighteenth out of nineteen children, of whom only twelve survived birth, Sebastião Rodrigues Maia was born in Tijuca on September 28, 1942. Just over the hills and past São Conrado beach from Rio de Janeiro's iconic beaches of Leblon, Ipanema, and Copacabana, Tijuca was a young neighborhood, full of immigrants, a bustling multiethnic lower-middle-class neighborhood where Tim's family made a decent living delivering boxed lunches to retirees and running a boarding house. As soon as Tim was old enough, he began delivering lunches, which is where he picked up his first nickname "Tião Marmiteiro."[1] Tim was a horrible delivery boy, as he would make regular detours to play with friends, neglecting his rigid delivery schedule. Tim's first job foreshadowed not only his inability to take direction, but also his insatiable appetite, as his expanding waist size betrayed his regular habit of snacking on the meals he was meant to deliver.

A musical prodigy, Tim was singing by age eight, enrolled in a music academy by twelve, and at the age of fourteen formed his first band, Os Tijucanos do Ritmo (The Rhythmic Tijucans), with his childhood buddy and an unsung hero of the Brazilian soul scene, Edson Trindade. Tim was the first among his friends in the neighborhood to learn to play guitar, so he taught the other members of the Matoso Street gang (named after the street in the neighborhood where they would gather to hang out and play music), including future Brazilian superstars Roberto Carlos and Erasmo Esteves (later known as Erasmo Carlos). Even a young Jorge Ben Jor was known to hang out in the neighborhood devouring American rock n' roll and the new revolutionary bossa nova sound with equal enthusiasm. Tim and Erasmo even referred to each other as "Tim Jobim" and "Erasmo Gilberto" in reference to the rising bossa nova stars Antonio Carlos "Tom" Jobim and João Gilberto.

Tim's second band was far more successful. The Sputniks included Erasmo on guitar and Tim on drums. The band gained the attention of rock n' roll impresario Carlos Imperial, who put them on his TV shows, *Clube Do Rock* (Rock Club) on TV Tupi starting in 1958 and *Os Brotos Comandam* (The Youngsters In Command) on TV Continental, starting in 1959. The show featured live performances by the best of Rio's musical youth, including many of the Matoso gang and many other soon-to-be stars of the *Jovem Guarda* (The Young Guard) scene. On Imperial's next show *Clube Do Rock*, the Snakes (Erasmo's next band without Tim) backed Roberto Carlos, doing his best Elvis Presley, and Tim Maia, doing his best Little Richard.[2]

Eduardo Araújo, who would later be of great of help to Tim, had recently arrived in Rio de Janeiro to perform on one of *Clube Do Rock*'s final shows. "He was already Tim Maia," Eduardo remembers, "because Carlos Imperial changed everyone's name, except for me. He showed up Sebastião Rodrigues Maia and Carlos Imperial said, 'Sebastião Rodrigues Maia won't be a success anywhere. Starting today, you're Tim Maia, nobody will forget Tim Maia.'"[3] Sadly, they did, or better said, they never had a real opportunity to know this future star as Imperial's efforts to sell American-style rock n' roll fell flat, at least initially.

The death of Tim's father in 1959, the breakup of the Sputniks, and the canceling of Imperial's show made it clear to the young Tim that he needed to find a new scene. He had always talked about traveling to the United States, but his father had been vehemently anti-American, so with nothing left to keep him in Tijuca, he planned his escape to the United States. Tim saved money and convinced the naïve neighborhood priest to cover what he lacked, while lying to the immigration officials that he was participating in an exchange program to study television production in New York. He arrived in New York City in 1959 with no one to greet him, unable to speak a word of English, only seventeen years old, and with twelve dollars in his pocket.

Tim's only plan was to find a family friend who had married an American and was now living in Tarrytown, New York, in Westchester County, a thirty-minute train ride from Grand Central Station. Tim made his way up the Hudson to the home of the O'Meara family, who had no idea Tim was coming, and they reluctantly hosted him until he found a place of his own. However, Tim never really got his own place, preferring to couch-surf with friends and fellow musicians. While Carlos Imperial may have already dubbed him "Tim," while in the United States he traded the difficult-to-pronounce *Tião* [pronounced: "*chee-ow*"] for Jimmy. Over the next four years, Tim worked as a pizza delivery boy, a short-order cook, a janitor at an insane asylum, and a snow shoveler. As he would recall later in life, "I took my course in *malandragem*[4] and drugs in the U.S. I learned everything fast there because everyone snorts, smokes pot, screws, drinks booze and pops pills."[5]

One wonders why Tim stayed in the sleepy town up the river from Harlem, Brooklyn, The Bronx, and countless opportunities for a young and ambitious musicians to take root. I think the answer was that he was able to find just what he needed right in town and within reach. A sixteen-year-old Roger Bruno met Tim not long after the Brazilian arrived in Tarrytown and invited him to join his fledgling R&B group built around four singers, the Ideals. Roger recalls that the five-member vocal group came together effortlessly: "There was something about Tim where he and I musically related, so we got to be really good friends, and then we started writing, and then we wrote 'New Love,' which was, like, the second song I ever wrote." The song, which was later recorded for Tim's fourth solo album more than ten years later in 1973, was a mix of R&B and bossa nova. "He turned me

Figure 2 *Left to right: Roger Bruno, Frank Delmerico, Tim Maia, and Felix DeMasi. Photo courtesy of Roger Bruno.*

on to João Gilberto," Roger remembers. "He was a real João freak, and it was about the time when bossa nova was hitting in the States, and we wanted to do something with bossa and pop music. So, we wrote that song and decided to do a demo on it."[6] The song only exists as an acetate in Bruno's possession, but beyond it being Tim's very first "professional" recording session, it's notable for featuring Brazil's most famous drummer at that time, Milton Banana, who happened to be in town for the legendary bossa nova concert at Carnegie Hall.[7] Notable session player, Don Payne, played bass. Tim played acoustic guitar and sang backup vocals to Roger's lead vocal.

Who knows what might have happened if the Ideals had actually stuck together long enough to shop around their demo. Roger reminisced about their teenage daydreams of headlining the Apollo and all the adoring female fans, but he also remembers that Tim's talents weren't just limited to making music: "Let's just say he always had a way to make money. Believe me, Tim was an outlaw." In 1963, Tim was arrested in Daytona Beach, Florida, with some black American friends. The cops pulled over their stolen car and found the deviants in possession of marijuana. Tim was sent to jail for six months before being deported back to Brazil. Roger Bruno remembers receiving a phone call from Tim in jail, which wasn't the first time, but this time he was in Florida and enough was enough. "He was very unhappy that we didn't bail him out," Roger recalls. "For him, that was it. His hopes for a career in the U.S. were gone."

Having spent most of the North American winter in jail, Tim arrived back in Brazil in April 1964. He landed in Rio de Janeiro during a period of tremendous political turmoil, just days following

Figure 3 *Left to right: Roger Bruno, Felix DeMasi, Tim Maia, Paul Mitranga, and Bill Adair. Photo courtesy of Roger Bruno.*

the right-wing military coup that toppled the progressive, democratically elected President Goulart.[8] Not entirely unlike the bleeding heartbreak following JFK's assassination in 1963, Brazil's doe-eyed liberals and bossa nova romantics experienced a similar existential loss as they watched their country being taken over by a US-backed military dictatorship. For the next twenty-one years, Brazil was ruled by a succession of military leaders with extralegal kidnappings, detentions, assassinations, and—what every musician had to worry about—censorship. During those decades Brazilians saw the degree of oppression wax and wane according to the various military leaders' levels of morality, but the early to mid-1970s were known as some of the worst years. But unlike some repressive dictatorships, Brazil's military leaders avoided interfering too much with the fundamentals of Brazilian life: Catholicism and samba.

What better to distract the populace from the extralegal activities of its government than with ephemeral pop culture. Just as Tim arrived home, Tim's old friends from Tijuca made a splash in the wake of Beatlemania that swept through Brazil (and the world) in 1963–4. "Even soft water hitting a hard rock can make a hole," Eduardo Araújo says, calling upon an old Brazilian adage to describe the *Jovem Guarda's* eventual triumph over the media blockade that shut down *Clube Do Rock* and kept the nascent Brazilian rock n' roll scene momentarily at bay. "But then all of a sudden, the radio stations started to play it . . . ." Eduardo's career took off and so too did those of Tim's old friends, Roberto Carlos and Erasmo Esteves, now going by Erasmo Carlos.

Tim returned to Brazil with only the clothes on his back. He called his mother from the airport to pick him up, telling his family and friends that he came back to Brazil in order to avoid being drafted to fight in Vietnam. Before he could even get a plan together, he was already in trouble again. Hanging out with an old friend, they decided to steal some nice furniture they noticed left unattended in front of a house. Moments later, the neighbor came outside and started screaming, "thieves, they're stealing the furniture." While his buddy escaped, Tim was caught trying to run away with a chair on his head. Within weeks of getting out of a US jail he was back in jail, now in Rio de Janeiro. "You can't imagine what you pick up in jail in Brazil," Tim said about this time in jail in Rio. "I got picked up and did a year in there and I am still traumatized by [those prison] uniforms until today."[9] Tim rarely shied away from talking about his life, the good, the bad, and the hilarious, but he rarely (and never in public, aside from the above quote) spoke about this year he spent in jail in Rio de Janeiro. Certainly, more brutal and twice as long as his stint in the Florida jail, sitting in his jail cell Tim couldn't be further from his dream of headlining the Apollo Theater back in New York. But rather than let his demoralizing surroundings and string of bad luck kill his spirit, Tim emerged from the experience tougher and even more determined. Though it didn't help that his cellmates and guards were as incredulous when Tim claimed that he'd taught the fresh pop stars Roberto and Erasmo Carlos how to play guitar.

With his old buddies from the Matoso gang dominating the pop airwaves as the leading lights of the *Jovem Guarda* scene, it was clear to Tim that Rio de Janeiro was not the place to stage his assault on the Brazilian recording industry. The *Jovem Guarda*'s ground zero was São Paulo. "I lived in the United States from 1959 to 1964," Tim told journalist Ruy Castro in Brazil's *Playboy* in 1991.

> When I returned, the *Jovem Guarda* was already armed. I got myself into trouble; I was arrested and put in jail for a year. When I got out of the can, them—my old gang—didn't even want to look at me—"Look it's Tião here! Look it's Tião Maconheiro [Tim pothead]" I stayed for three years in São Paulo trying to do the *Jovem Guarda* [thing], but they wouldn't let me in. . . . I was sabotaged by Roberto Carlos and his gang all that time. They were afraid of soul music—later I came to conclude. At that time, I never imagined that I, chubby, mulatto, would compete with them, they were the kings of *Jovem Guarda* [laughs].[10]

Tim's determination to bring the sound and spirit of soul music to Brazil was initially a liability because no one was singing this music. Eventually, Erasmo got him a single on his label, Fermata, Tim's debut release from 1968, "What You Want To Bet" backed with "These Are The Songs." Laercio de Freitas, a revered Afro-Brazilian pianist, composer, and arranger was hired by the label for the session. "Tim was a crazy man," Laercio recalls during an interview in San Diego, California, in 2017. "I knew him since I was working in São Paulo," Laercio digs back into his memories of Tim's first professional session. "The band was playing the song [in the studio] and he enters, 'you guys didn't think I was coming did you?' A good person, Tim had a good soul, a good spirit."[11]

The single tanked, as did another on Roberto's label (CBS) from 1969, "Meu Pais" backed with "Sentimento." That same year, Roberto recorded Tim's song "Não Vou Ficar," an upbeat and defiant funk vamp, which became a huge hit. Tim's old friend from the *Clube Do Rock* days, Eduardo Araújo, was the one who passed the song to Roberto. A part of the São Paulo–based *Jovem Guarda* scene, but with a grittier rock image, Eduardo's career was going like gangbusters and he generously pulled the homeless and struggling Tim under his wing. "When he lived with me in the Hotel Danube for a long time, he was a guy rejected by everybody, all of the musicians, the producers, everyone judged him because he had been in jail," Eduardo said. "When he showed up, I received him with open arms. He didn't need for the basic things in life living in the Presidential Suite of the Hotel Danube with me."

When Tim re-entered Eduardo's life, and now his apartment as well, the original rocker from the *Jovem Guarda* scene was looking to try something new. Tim suggested this new style from the United States that he was trying to sing: soul music. "Nobody was listening to it," Eduardo insists. "They were all imported records, they didn't sell here or play on the radio." Eduardo's record label was understandably nervous about this idea, but ultimately Odeon relented. The assistant producer would be a certain Tim Maia. Soul music could only be heard at select nightclubs in Brazil's biggest cities. The Cave club in São Paulo was the only place in town to dig the primordial funk wafting down from the United States. "The nightclubs were first, they played: Arthur Conley, Aretha Franklin, James Brown," Eduardo remembers. "Tim knew this spot on Rua Augusta and all the records were imported, and we bought everything to listen to. It took us six months to put together the material [for the album]," Eduardo remembers. Eduardo's album, *A Onda É Boogaloo* (The Wave is Boogaloo) (Odeon, 1969), didn't make Tim a star, but he learned a lot about the record making process. The album, "wasn't a big success but it opened the doors for Tim Maia … and when he left there [Hotel Danube], he was already a star."

Milton Miranda, the legendary producer at Odeon wanted to sign Tim for a recording contract, but with Tim Maia's uncanny ability to create chaos, he misread the contract and threw a temper tantrum and was escorted out of the building. Thankfully, Tim was good at making friends like the three *paulista* teens soon to be known as Os Mutantes. Lead guitarist and youngest Dias brother, Sérgio, remembers that

> there were a bunch of guys [musicians] in this hit parade [television show], in terms of musical styles and that's where we met Tim. He had just arrived from America, so when he started to sing, we were so into the Four Tops and all those guys, we knew all the backing vocals. So, every time he would sing, we did the backing vocals. So, when we went to Polydor, we introduced him [to our label, Polydor].[12]

André Midani, the head of Phillips/Polydor was on the lookout for new talent, asking his acts if they knew of any talented unsigned musicians. Evidently, both Erasmo Carlos, who'd just signed with Philips in 1969 and the Paulista teens, Os Mutantes, answered without hesitation, saying the same thing, "Tim Maia, very crazy, but brilliant!" With those words of caution, Midani deputized his new producer, Manoel Barenbein who had come over to Philips from RGE in 1967, to track down Tim. "So Manoel looked for the mysterious artist from house to house, until one day Tim appeared, signed with us and entered the studio to deliver his first hit, 'Primavera.'"[13] Eduardo Araújo also takes credit for making the introduction to Barenbein, making it at least five people who have claimed credit for getting Tim signed to Polydor; let's just agree it was a group effort. As a multinational record label and one of Brazil's premier imprints, Tim was ready to launch his assault on hundreds of thousands of Brazilian ears.

Before "Primavera" hit, Nelson Motta, who was then an A&R man, producer, and general musical impresario, was working on a new album for beloved singer Elis Regina. He was looking for new material when Tim's producer Jairo Pires made the introduction. Elis fell in love with Tim's English-Portuguese hybrid from his first single, "These Are the Songs," and instead of just covering the song, she invited him to join her on the track as a duet, released on her 1970 album *Em Pleno Verão* (Philips, 1970). Motta recognized the importance of this bold new voice:

Here was something absolutely new. Until then Brazilian music was divided into nationalist M.P.B. [Musica Popular Brasileira, a catch-all acronym, meaning "Brazilian Popular Music" that mostly referred to sophistocated pop music from the late 1960s and

1970s], *Tropicalismo* and international rock. All really white and really English. Tim Maia changed the game, introducing modern Black music from the U.S. to national pop music, linking funk and *baião*, bringing soul closer to bossa nova and opening windows and doors to new forms of music that were not tropicalist, nor M.P.B,, nor rock n' roll: they were quintessentially Brazilian. They were Tim Maia.[14]

Tim's first single on Polydor, "Primavera" (Spring) was a runaway hit, as was his debut album *Tim Maia* (Polydor, 1970). The album sold 210,000 copies and stayed at the top position of Rio de Janeiro's album charts for twenty-four straight weeks.[15] Tim's vocal style, like that of Elis Regina and another young singer, Milton Nascimento, abandoned the hushed tones of bossa nova, preferring a more dramatic and soaring delivery reminiscent of older vocal styles, such as the samba *canção* and boleros of the 1950s. Of course, Tim's central influences were his soul music heroes James Brown, Wilson Pickett, Curtis Mayfield, and Ronnie Isely of the Isely Brothers. In addition to introducing a new style with a bold new voice, Tim's earliest albums overflowed with swinging, soulful songs, composed by Tim and his immediate circle, including soul supporters Eduardo Araújo, Cassiano and his brother, Camarão, Fábio, Edson Trindade (from his first group Os Tijucanos do Ritmo), and Hyldon. Tim's first album turned Tim into the star he always dreamed he would become.

Three more albums followed in 1971, 1972, and 1973, all self-titled; collectively they form the bedrock of Brazilian soul music. Like the best purveyors of diasporic soul music, Tim's amalgamation of R&B with domestic traditions was effortless. In spite of Tim's popular and critical success, loads of money, bottomless whiskey bottles, endless joints, and hordes of adoring female fans, he always wanted more. In his quest to find a deeper truth, or at least a laugh, Tim experimented with every drug imaginable, and even tried to "open the minds" of the uptight employees at his record label, Philips, the parent company of Polydor (which he dubbed "Flips"), with a sheet of L.S.D. that he brought back from London. Tim approached each and every Philips employee, beginning with the accounting department, which needed more immediate "salvation," asking, "Do you know what this is? This here is a divine gift that will open your mind, improve your life and make you happier. It doesn't have side effects, it's non-addictive and it won't make your hair fall out—it only does good. It's called L.S.D. and you take it like this."[16]

Tim was a regular drug user, particularly of marijuana, which he asserted had saintly effects of peace and artistic inspiration. When recording at Philips, everyone knew when Tim was on break, because the smell of marijuana wafting out of the air vents betrayed his favorite joint-smoking spot—the central air conditioner room. But this was classic Tim Maia: even when he was taking a break, he was creating a scene. Ed Motta, Tim's nephew and the heir to his uncle's physique and soulful style, was a young child during Tim's early career, but he remembers that

> the first time I listened to American funk music and saw the characters and the atmosphere of soul music, that just looked to me like my uncle Tim and his friends. He was freaky, very wild, always doing drugs and having crazy sex. Because of his lifestyle, my family would tell me he's everything you can't be in your life.[17]

2 The Band, the Shed, and Fatherhood (Late 1973–Early 1974)

As the canary in the coalmine for Brazilian soul, Tim blazed his own trail, but he couldn't control how the music industry and Brazilian public commodified his version of American soul music. While Brazilian pop and rock singers and groups wholesale adopted the instruments, drugs, fashion, and lifestyle of American and British rockers, Tim was still categorized as a solo vocalist, not unlike a Tom Jones. "He liked that band scene," Paulinho Guitarra says.

> At that time, he didn't have that desire to be a star; he wanted to be part of a band, a team. He didn't like rock, but he loved the rock n' roll approach and lifestyle. He loved the climate and atmosphere of rock n' roll. He would say, "Shit, man the rock n' roll bands in São Paulo are totally organized. They have roadies that set everything up and make sure everything's right. They have all the best equipment, Fender guitars, Gibsons. Us singers here [in Rio] don't have anything."

The self-contained soul and funk bands that Tim idolized from the United States, like the Isely Brothers, Earth, Wind & Fire or the Ohio Players didn't exist yet in Brazil, but he was about to change that. Whether it was his intention or just a gravitational phenomenon beyond his control, Tim attracted (and in the case of Don Pi, abducted) talented, young musicians activated by the exciting and funky sounds heard on Tim's records and the few soul artists played on countercultural radio shows like that of pioneering radio personality, Newton Duarte a.k.a. "Big Boy."

Encouraged by his old friend Tibério Gaspar to set up his own production company, Seroma Productions was born. Recording and producing his recordings independently, Tim controlled the process and made more money. Most importantly, now he had 100 percent control over his recordings, down to every last musician. Beginning in 1972 and moving into 1973 Tim relied less and less on session musicians provided, or recommended, by his record label or producer. Paulinho Guitarra was one of the first musicians to become a fixture in Tim's crew, joining at age seventeen, having been playing professionally since he was thirteen. A soft-spoken, short, skinny, white kid from Niterói, just across the bay from Rio, Paulinho was a guitar wunderkind and one of Tim's band's earliest and most consistent secret weapons.

Serginho Trombone (trombone, keyboards), Oberdan Magalhães (sax), and Luiz Carlos Batera (drums) all graduated from Dom Salvador's Abolição band after Salvador extended his vacation in New York to permanent. The dissolution of this magnificent band (one that had pioneered a fusion of jazz, soul, funk, and Afro-Brazilian elements) resulted in available talent for Tim to absorb into his orbit as early as 1972 as all three appear on Tim's third self-titled album released the same year.

Another musician who went on to a successful solo career was Carlos Dafé, a short, wiry piano player, who later revealed himself to be a fantastic singer, making up for technical ability with plenty of soul. "More than musicians and friends, Paulinho Guitarra and Dafé would become like *cambonos*[1] for Tim, serving him like devotees of a saint," Nelson Motta writes. "They bought him his meals and alcohol, they ran errands, they were company when he needed it, they helped him with it all. The other musicians felt a little jealous but did not have the patience of these two to deal with Tim's turbulent lifestyle."[2]

There is a long tradition of Brazilian musicians incorporating their main instrument into their performing name like Jackson do Pandeiro (tambourine), Jacob do Bandolim (mandolin), Chico Batera (drums), or Dino de Sete Cordas (seven-string guitar), but Tim Maia baptized and re-baptized a large percentage of the musicians who passed through his band. Few band leaders took this naming convention to the same extreme as Tim, as he announced his band from a 1974 concert in São Paulo: "On horns, my friend, Paulinho Trompete number one, and my other friend, Paulinho Trompete number two."[3] In order to really keep them straight, Tim gave them additional nicknames, Paulinho *Ganso* (Martins was called "goose" because of his long neck) and Paulinho *Figado* (de Oliveira was called "liver," because he frequently complained about his health).

Paulinho remembers when Tim announced that the whole band was going to see *Wattstax*, the concert film/documentary featuring the musical stars of Stax Records, most notably Isaac Hayes, one of Tim's favorites according to Paulinho. "Around the same time, I think there was the album and movie by Joe

Cocker—*Mad Dogs and Englishmen*. 'Come on band, let's go see Joe Cocker!' Those were the two films he took the whole band to see." But before you get confused, Tim Maia did not like rock music. Paulinho remembers him often saying, "it's a white thing."

In 1973, Tim bought a large plot of land on a hill called Sacopã behind the Rodrigo de Freitas Lagoon, the large body of water in the lowlands behind Copacabana, Ipanema, and Leblon beaches before the city gains altitude quickly climbing the steep slopes up to the famous Christ statue, *Cristo de Redentor*. The plot was wedged between a nature preserve and a large and mostly wild municipal park; Tim's property was at the top of Sacopã Street where its name changes to Vitória Régia. Still undeveloped real estate at the time, it had panoramic views of the Rodrigues de Freitas Lagoon, *Cristo Redentor*, and the Ipanema and Leblon beaches. Around them, just some tall grass and undeveloped lots along the slope. Tim recruited his band to build a rudimentary structure with two rooms, one to be the headquarters of his music publishing company (Seroma) and the other, a rehearsal space for the Seroma band.

The Seroma headquarters, or the shed (*O Barracão*) as it would come to be known, was built entirely of wood. "I was one of the few people that could go there to Seroma when he was rehearsing, to play with them," Tim's close friend and a crucial musician in the growing Brazilian soul scene, Hyldon, explains:

Tim built his Seroma studio on Vitória Régia Street based on a record of mine by Lee Michaels [*Barrel*, 1970 A&M records]. It's a great record, this album that I bought in the United States; it was a gatefold album with a cabin on the cover made totally of wood. I showed it to Tim . . . and I never got that record back, did

I? I lost that record. He made the studio based on the cover of that record, just like the photo, completely of wood.[4]

This album proved so influential to Tim, his second and third solo albums from 1971 and 1972 in their original deluxe gatefold editions feature collages of photos across their gatefold sleeves clearly inspired by *Barrel*'s design and layout.

Tim wanted a place to escape to, where he could rehearse at any hour and have enough space for his menagerie of dogs (later reaching up to thirty-two canines), too many for his main residency, a luxury apartment in Copacabana. The shed had two main rooms and a small kitchen with only the most basic plumbing and electricity. "He put a mattress and some pillows in one room and filled the [larger] room with guitars, *tumbadoras*, drums, amplifiers, microphones, Hammond organ, electric piano and a soundboard," Nelson Motta describes.

> The boys—some of the best musicians of Rio: Luiz Carlos Batera, Paulinho Guitarra, Serginho Trombone and saxophonist Oberdan Magalhães—played all day. Junior Mendes, Solange and Viviane did the backing vocals like the Black back-up singers from Motown. Two huge dogs roamed free in the yard, the German Shepherd Kaleche and Dick, a Brazilian Mastiff, the size of a calf, with whom Tim had great affinity. The sessions were long, but no musician left before Tim finished the rehearsal and secured the dogs.[5]

But there was just one problem with the shed, as Hyldon explains: "[Tim] built the studio half on his land, half on his neighbor's land," in his rush to complete the project. One day

Hyldon visited Tim at Seroma, shortly after receiving the horrible news from the neighbor whose land half of the shed sat on. "They're gonna cut my studio in half," Tim told Hyldon, furious with the company that gave him notice, Aveplan. "I'm gonna write a samba, a revenge song and it's gonna be a huge hit, I'm gonna really fuck them!"

> *Aveplan é maldosa* [Aveplan is evil]
>
> *Aveplan é gulosa* [Aveplan is gluttonous]
>
> *Aveplan* (mumbles)
>
> *Cuidado Aveplan!* [Watch out Aveplan][6]

Tim's real estate revenge song never materialized, but the shed was demolished, and another studio was built squarely on his property where the jam sessions resumed as soon as possible.

In 1973, Tim also finally got to return to the United States, ten years after his inglorious deportation, visiting New York City for a couple weeks, where rumor has it he rehearsed with James Brown's backing band, the J.B.'s. My research could not confirm these mythical sessions mentioned by Philips/Polydor honcho André Midani in his memoir.[7] Paulinho Guitarra is certain the jam session never happened "because he would have talked about it and he said nothing about it. He never said anything to me about it and we lived together, we were together all the time. It could be that André [Midani] planned something or he had the intention, but it didn't happen."

Before departing for New York, Paulinho asked Tim to "'buy me a Gibson SJ like the one Santana has,' but I didn't get it and instead he brought [for himself] a white German shepherd."

Figure 4 *Postcard sent by Tim Maia in 1973 to Paulinho Guitarra. From the archive of Paulinho Guitarra.*

Paulinho does have definitive proof of Tim's return to the United States in 1973 in the form of a postcard from Tim with a photo of a typical mid-century Times Square scene with the following words inscribed to his friend:

> Hello, hello Master Paulo,
>
> Here everything is cool. I'm trying to bring the Altec amplifiers. I got to see everybody, and it was a nice surprise. I bought a German Shepherd named Clyde [spelled "CLAID"]. I'm bringing him home with me and in a little I'll be there.
>
> Until then, a hug
>
> Tim Maia[8]

In 1973, the shed was the unofficial headquarters of the nascent Brazilian soul music scene and a daily meeting place for friends

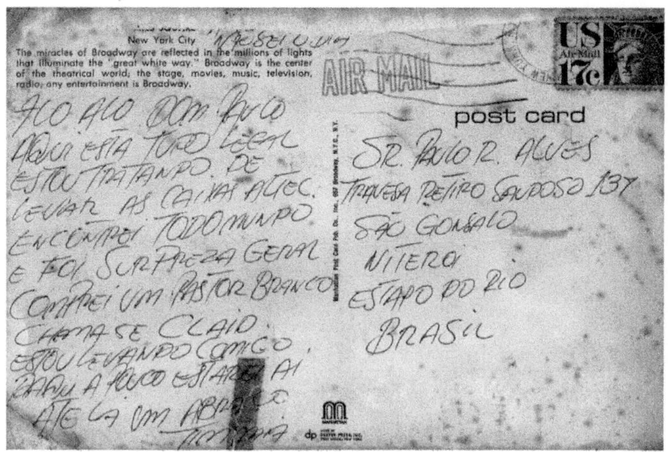

Figure 5 *Postcard sent by Tim Maia in 1973 to Paulinho Guitarra. From the archive of Paulinho Guitarra.*

of Tim's like Brazilian soul's two princes Cassiano and Hyldon, Tim's bandleader and right-hand man Paulinho Guitarra, lyricist Tibério Gaspar, and any number of the rotating cast of Tim's go-to studio and live gig musicians. "[It was] the cradle of Brazilian soul music," Paulinho Guitarra reminisces. "Every musician, Serginho Trombone, Oberdan, these soul, jazz, musicians of that time floated around Tim Maia, like mosquitos, ever present, ready to play if [Tim] needed them." Looking at photos with Paulinho in his apartment in Niterói, he comments:

> What a beautiful photo, me and my idol, Robson Jorge. For me, he was the best Brazilian musician of all time. He was a couple years older than me and started playing professionally, like me very young, but a few years before me. [He was a] great bass player, fantastic keyboard player, and an intergalactic

guitarist! . . . We called him Jorge Robson because Tim always called him Jorginho and only later Tim learned that his first name was Robson, so from then on, he [still] called him "Jorge Robson" instead of "Robson Jorge."

Some musicians, like Oberdan Magalhães, Serginho Trombone, and Robson Jorge, who were becoming increasingly in demand for outside session work, came and went on their own schedules, while others were subject to Tim's exacting expectations at daily rehearsals: "That harmony is wrong! That solo was crap! Get the fuck out of here, I don't want to ever see you again," Paulinho Guitarra imitates Tim during a typical rehearsal. "And then maybe one month later, 'hey Tim, you got some smoke, man?' and then Tim says, 'sure, let's play some music, you should come back to the band . . .'. Like flies flying around . . . I was the only one that never came and went. I stayed until I left for good. When I left [in 1977], I left."

With most of the key variables now firmly in his control, from the handpicked and rigorously rehearsed musicians, to the twenty-four-hour Seroma rehearsal space, Tim Maia wrote and rehearsed the songs for his fourth long-player. The constant flow of musicians and songwriters meant that Tim had first pick of some of the best songs coming out of his group of friends and when he was ready to play some music, which was daily, all he had to do was show up and a band assembled around him. It was here, at the shed, that Tim Maia worked and reworked the songs for his fourth studio album. Maybe in reaction to the less-than-hysterical response to his third album or inspired by his newfound musical autonomy composing and rehearsing on his own timeline at the Seroma studios, Tim delivered his best album yet, and possibly his best career album.

As much as I love Brazilian soul music, some of it (basically everything prior to 1973, with a few exceptions) retains a cutesy, cloying mimicry of tougher and more soulful American sides, like a Tom Jones cover of Sam & Dave—still funky, but stiff at times and I don't mean to pick on Mr. Jones, who's cool, but has never been hip. Tim's first three albums, while all classics, have this problem in their weaker moments, but that's where things changed with his fourth album. Just as Eduardo Araújo and Tim struggled to assemble a band capable of playing the soul and funk tunes for Eduardo's *A Onda É Boogaloo*, the coaching and directing of the Brazilian musicians took time and familiarity.

Tim's dreams became reality by 1973 with the release of his fourth solo album on Polydor, *Tim Maia* (Polydor, 1973). This album made Tim Maia one of Brazil's biggest stars with the hits, "Gostava Tanto de Você" (I Liked You So Much) and "Réu Confesso" (I Confess), among many now-classic album tracks. The cover of this, yet another self-titled Tim Maia album—excepting the Rational albums, all six of his other albums between 1970 and 1977 are self-titled—shows Tim posing outside (presumably behind the Seroma studios) wearing a blue denim shirt over a blue collared shirt with a silver medallion hanging mid-chest. Even a quick glance at the covers of Tim's first four self-titled albums from 1970, 1971, 1972 and this one from 1973 gives the appearance of an annual time-lapse film with each successive cover showing Tim getting fatter and hairier. By this album from 1973, his afro is substantial, and his beard is omnipresent, yet still patchy.

This album is the first of a succession of albums that makes sure to note on the LP jacket or insert that the album was "rehearsed at the Seroma studios," excepting the two Rational albums whose LP jacket real estate was taken up by Rational Culture diagrams. Tim's albums were generally sparse on details, but this fact, he made a point of noting on every album beginning with his fourth album, *Tim Maia* (Polydor, 1973) through *Tim Maia* (Som Livre, 1977). During these four years (1973–7) Tim released six albums, one single, and recorded twenty-seven minutes' worth of unreleased Rational material.

Despite his reputation later in life, Tim loved performing and if you caught him on a good night, legend has it, he was the best. Tim and the Seroma Band hit the road, devastating dance floors and inspiring baby making from Rio Grande Do Sul to Bahia. It was on one of these weekend tours where Tim spotted a young kid, a dead-ringer for a Brazilian Michael Jackson, who was fronting the opening band at a show in the small town of Barra Mansa, a few hours outside of Rio de Janeiro. Reginaldo Francisco was just a teenager, seventeen years old, energetic, charismatic and entrepreneurial as the leader of a highly successful local dance band. As he was still underage, his dad accompanied him to gigs, just as he had to this one when they were both invited to meet with Tim backstage. Despite his father's initial rebuff, young Reginaldo appealed to his musician mother, who conceded, signing away custody of the teen to one of the most notorious party animals in all of Brazil. Naturally, it was Tim who re-baptized Reginaldo as Don Pi, loosely translating to "Sir Keys."

It wouldn't be necessary to go into his love life, except for that Tim's tumultuous personal affairs factor significantly in his strange behavior beginning in early 1974. After his initial success in 1970, he met a lovely brunette Carioca named Janete with whom Tim, "started a passionate and turbulent romance, fueled by whiskey, acid, joints and punctuated by countless fights, breakups and vows of eternal love," Nelson Motta writes in *Vale Tudo*.[9] Starting in 1971 and lasting on-again, off-again for a year or more, Janete and Tim's fights and breakups started to outnumber their good times and eventually Janete left Tim sometime between his third and fourth albums. But Tim didn't stay single for too long. "Geisa [pronounced 'Gay-sah'] was an indigenous type of light-skinned woman, very cute, seventeen years-old, whose given name was Maria de Jesus Gomes da Silva," Nelson Motta writes.

> [It] ended soon with her disappearance to Campos [in Rio de Janeiro state about four hours away by car], in love with a soccer player, leaving Tim devastated . . . to try to escape the pain, Tim composed compulsively, full of new music, romantic and swinging tunes, funk and soul mixed with samba and seasoned with Latin and Caribbean flavors. The soul master's recipe was infallible.[10]

Out of nowhere, his cherished girlfriend Geisa returned to him, around April 1974, with her infant son, Márcio Leonardo (a.k.a. Léo Maia) in tow. The baby was the love child of Geisa and Jorge Vitório, a famous goalkeeper for the Fluminense soccer club. Márcio Leonardo was born on March 11, 1974, in Campos, Rio de Janeiro state and returned to Rio de Janeiro shortly after his birth with his mother who begged Tim to take her back. "But Tim was so happy with the return of Geisa that he forgave her," Nelson Motta writes:

> He was as happy as if he was the actual father. He called his friends and celebrated drinking whiskey and distributing cigars.

The [boy's] name was chosen by Tim, Márcio Leonardo, [named after the] composer of [one of Tim's big hits] "A Festa Dos Santo Reis." . . . He waited on Geisa hand on foot and the old flame reignited their passion.[11]

The flame stayed lit for maybe a month before Geisa took off yet again. "When she left, she was already pregnant with Carmelo, and she came back two or three weeks later," Don Pi (who was now living with Tim full time) remembers.

It was a hard time, because it was between the beginning of the Rational [Culture] thing and Tim was upside down, really confused about the whole thing; it all happened at once. And then she came back to say that she was pregnant and that she was worried about Márcio Leonardo [who she had left behind with Tim and Pi]. And I remember the conversation when she said she was pregnant from him, and he said, "are you sure? . . . you gotta be kidding me! I already assumed fatherhood for one kid, and now you come back after being gone for a month and say that it's my kid?"

Tim eventually accepted her story and embraced the in-utero child as his own. "It was his big dream," Nelson Motta writes. "If, with Léo, who wasn't his son, he had discovered such affection and paternal [instincts], with the birth of his heir, blood of his blood, his happiness would be complete."[12]

Following his fourth hit album in as many years for Polydor, Tim was one of the biggest stars in Brazilian music, so, naturally he decided to push his luck with the executives of Polydor's parent company, Philips. He demanded that his next record be a double album, after all it was the 1970s. Philips chief André Midani knew that Tim was equal parts gold mine and liability and released him from his contract, a ballsy move at the time given Tim's track record until that point. RCA Victor's Brazilian subsidiary gave Tim his desired double album and something like $300,000 as a signing bonus. Don Pi recalls: "It was a lot of money." Influenced by his friend and fellow professional musician Tibério Gaspar, Tim designed his contract with RCA so that he would self-produced the album under his own production company, Seroma, and RCA would commit to buy the final product.

"Tim and his band took over the RCA studios, deep in a dark gallery full of shops including hairdressers, handbag and bikini factories and a weightlifting gym," Nelson Motta sets the scene. "The audio engineers trembled at the warning that Tim Maia was on his way, the artistic director received him at the door as a king and introduced him to all of the departments. There was the green light to start the double album of his dreams."[13] Recently remodeled and upholstered entirely in orange, with an eight-channel console, German microphones, full air-conditioning, and located in Botafogo just a few minutes from his apartment in Copacabana, Tim and band were in hi-fi heaven.

Regarding RCA's influence on these sessions, Don Pi recalls, "at the beginning [the producer] it was Guti [Graça Mello], but Tim basically was the producer because he was doing this record through his enterprise [Seroma] and selling [the final product] to RCA. So, there was not really a [RCA] producer there." The new RCA deal gave Tim 100 percent artistic control, allowing him to choose all of his musicians, and to record whenever he wanted for as long as he wanted, without any record company executives telling him what to do. Paulinho Trompete #1 (Paulo Roberto de Oliveira) described it as "a very collaborative recording process for the Rational records," noting that compared to previous recording sessions or the few later sessions he participated in, this was "the first time and the only time Tim recorded like this."[14]

"The artistic directors and the RCA's sales department were ecstatic with the first news of the recordings," Nelson Motta writes.[15] Tim's vision for his album wouldn't be complete though without a certain sound, something he and Paulinho couldn't get enough of: Ernie Isely's guitar sound from the latest Isely Brothers record *3+3* (RCA/T-Neck, 1973). Per Tim's request, Paulinho tracked down the closest thing he could find to Ernie Isely's phaser pedal. "I had a phaser-type thing," Paulinho says, "It was difficult at that time to find a phaser in Brazil. I found a knock-off phaser that I used on the Rational albums." With the band rehearsed and kernels of songs already conceived at Seroma headquarters, Tim started 1974 wasting no time laying down a set of tracks. Paulinho Guitarra picks up the story:

> We went to the brand-new studio with brand new equipment and eight channels. We recorded lots of songs, recording and recording, from nine in the morning until nine at night, everybody playing and jamming lots of grooves all day long. The thing with these recordings is that Tim would record everything! We would be playing and he'd come in, "record it!" We arrived at the studio, "let's record. Record everything, the conversations, the music, everything."

Don Pi had to go back to Barra Mansa to finish high school, so he missed some, but not all of the initial RCA sessions where these backing tracks for the double album were recorded.

> In this short time [after I arrived] before he jumped into Rational Culture, we were already in the studio to record the new record. . . . And then we started to record the backing tracks, because there were no lyrics yet, except for "Que Beleza" which already had lyrics, going, "Oof, oof, oof que beleza," but there was no mention of any Rational Culture things.

Tim's life was pretty crazy at that time, especially for Don Pi, a naïve young kid from a small town. "I graduated and then I decided not to continue my studies. The money was too good. With the money I was making [playing with Tim], to continue with school was senseless." Pi was likely excited and nervous to be returning to Rio to finish Tim's double album, running with the big boys and their big appetites for the rock n' roll lifestyle. Little did he know he would return to his boss and idol deeply engaged with a strange book and some bizarre ideas, the strangest being that there would be no more marijuana smoking, which was a shame because Pi was just starting to like it . . .

Interlude: Seu Manoel and Rational Culture

Many outsiders who are quite prepared to accept the sincerity of Moonies and Mormons throw up their hands at the thought of "crackpots" seriously believing that alien beings have come in flying saucers to bring mankind a message from the gods. But this is really no more unbelievable than the basis of many other religions. As the White Queen says to Alice, "Why, sometimes I've believed as many as six impossible things before breakfast."[1] Most people if they are prepared to be honest, do so—at least by lunch.

DAVID V. BARRETT, *THE NEW BELIEVERS*[2]

Manoel Jacintho Coelho was born in Rio de Janeiro in 1903 to musician parents of African descent. By thirteen, the young Coelho played the violin, but eventually settled on the seven-string guitar (a Brazilian model popular in samba and *choro* styles) as his preferred instrument. At eighteen he joined the Brazilian army, serving in the heavy machine-gun division. The early years of Coelho's life are referred to by his followers as his "true spiritual phase" beginning in 1928, at twenty-five years of age, when he opened an *Umbanda* (Afro-Brazilian religion) center that also treated the poor, hungry, and destitute, utilizing more than four hundred different herbal remedies.[3] By day

Coelho worked for Brazil's Foreign Ministry in Rio de Janeiro (then the capital of the country) and started a family, eventually numbering eight children. At thirty-two years of age on October 4, 1935, Manoel Jacintho Coelho became "disenchanted." On that day, he received the first of many communications from the "Rational World" that he subsequently transcribed to the page, eventually materializing as the *Universe in Disenchantment* book and later, a thousand-volume series of books.[4]

"The founder Manoel Jacintho Coelho was, on the day October 4, 1935, when he initiated communications with the Rational Superior, an *Umbanda* medium," writes Ricardo Neumann in his 2007 academic paper, "Cultura Racional e Letramento" (Rational Culture and Literacy). *Umbanda* is an indigenous Brazilian religion combining elements of *Macumba* (a catch-all name for African-influenced religions active in nineteenth-century Brazil), Roman Catholicism, and South American Indian religious traditions. Wikipedia tell us:

> Although some of its beliefs and most of its practices existed in the late 19th century in almost all of Brazil, it is assumed that *Umbanda* originated in Rio de Janeiro and surrounding areas in the early 20th century, mainly due to the work of a psychic (medium), Zéilio Fernandino de Moraes, who practiced *Umbanda* among the poor Afro-Brazilian population.[5]

Joseph A. Page, in his 1995 exploration of Brazilian culture and history, explains the key components and backstory of this uniquely Brazilian religion:

> *Umbanda* has traveled a torturous path. Its immediate roots date back to the 1850s, when a Frenchman who claimed to have

been possessed by a Druid spirit adopted the name Alain Kardec and wrote a number of books that launched a new spiritual cult. *Kardecism* was the highly rationalized belief in the existence of incorporeal beings in interplanetary space, and in the possibility of communicating with them. . . . *Kardecism* found fertile ground in Brazil, where it gained numerous converts during the late nineteenth and early twentieth centuries. Kardecists kept their distance from the Afro-Brazilian religions, which they considered a "low" form of spirituality. The white, middle-class Brazilians who joined the cult, however, gave it a new wrinkle. They shifted the focus to curing, so that spirits were summoned to alleviate members' physical as well as spiritual ills. . . . Kardecist mediums began to claim that they were summoning different kinds of spirits representing deeply rooted elements of Brazilian culture. From this trend emerged *Umbanda*, an intriguing projection of both Brazilianness and the nationalism that was gripping the country in the 1930s.[6]

Following President Vargas' revolution in 1930, Brazil underwent a period of tremendous economic and political growth, transforming the former Portuguese colony from a coffee and dairy economy into a modern nation with its own industrial infrastructure. In 1941, the Austrian writer Stefan Zweig gave Brazil the sub-title that continues to haunt and taunt South America's largest nation, forever the "country of the future."[7] Brazil is quite different than the United States when it comes to how our respective cultures have handled our relatively similar histories of mass slavery and racially based subjugation with its harmonious notion of itself as a "racial democracy." History, however, has shown us that Brazilian elites support the idea of diversity only so long as those in control stay white and European.

Coelho's Rio de Janeiro of the 1930s was no different with local elites celebrating the harmless and novel samba, while marginalizing the threatening or impure elements of Afro-Brazilian culture. Ricardo Neumann continues from his paper "Cultura Racional e Letramento": "These [groups], in the thirties, suffered under the intensification of the persecution of psychic religions. Fundamentally these were [religions] of African origin like *Candomblé* and *Umbanda*."

In this new and cosmopolitan Rio de Janeiro, Coelho and all of his spiritual brother and sisters were confronted with an existential crisis with three clear options: (1) abandon their spiritual pursuits; (2) go underground; or (3) evolve into a new religion more acceptable to the Eurocentric elites. With Rational Culture, Coelho wrapped his "African" *Umbanda* in scriptural doctrine to distance it from the ritualistic elements of the African and/or animist religions. Neumann writes:

> We can understand his attempt to escape the religious field in search for literacy as "salvation" as one of his strategies in creating Rational Culture. The reading of the volumes of *Universe in Disenchantment* as the only way to salvation is clearly linked to Manoel's targeting of a niche of the growing psychic religious market at the time, those followers of the mediumistic religions who wished to find a more literate psychic religious option, more "rationalized" and less connected to the ritual elements. Thus, we can see why the strategy behind the creation of Rational Culture is so intertwined with the idea of reading and literacy.[8]

Aside from its scriptural basis, another tenant of *Kardecism* that doesn't manifest as profoundly in *Umbanda* but was certainly picked up by Coelho with Rational Culture is the fundamental belief in intelligent and incorporeal life beyond Earth. Coelho founded Rational Culture in Rio de Janeiro shortly after his initial communication with the Rational Superior, first at his *Umbanda* Center in the working-class Rio de Janeiro neighborhood of Meier. Before long, he moved the movement's headquarters to the northern satellite city of Nova Iguaçu, initially based in a Moroccan-styled villa in the neighborhood of Belford Roxo. It was here that Tibério took Tim who first encountered the book *Universe in Disenchantment* at Tibério's house.

Tim Maia met a seventy-plus, towering (said to be nearly two meters tall, approximately 6 and a half feet tall) Afro-Brazilian gentlemen, worldly, musical, and seemingly endowed with supernatural powers and unknowable wisdom. It's rare to hear of Tim being intimidated or impressed by anybody, but Seu Manoel certainly left an impression on him. "I think he really needed something new in his life and he'd seen Seu Manoel do certain things, like levitate and even fly," Paulo Roberto de Oliveira (a.k.a. Paulinho Trompete #1) says. "I never saw it myself, but Tim talked about it. It was a new thing for Tim. How does someone levitate?" Even the academic Ricardo Neumann acknowledges Seu Manoel's mesmerizing appeal:

To observe the work of Manoel it's often inevitable to think, at least for a fraction of a second, that it's the diary of a madman. It is difficult to understand how a civil servant, *Umbanda* medium, thirty-one years old, can conceive of such treatises. How can someone who's not a fool . . . forge such a creation? This "explanation" for our nature, origin and destination, comes in very unusual ways. And that is where we must remember that Manoel was a medium of *Umbanda*, in that context in which he received, alongside the "messages" from the "Rational Superior," numerous influences from "*Umbanda* Intellectuals," Kardecists, Evolutionists, in short, a range of producers of meaning who prowled the religious field at the time.[9]

3 50 Mescaline + Universe in Disenchantment = Tim Maia Racional? (1974)

"In addition to the endless rehearsals [and recording sessions], in his spare time, Tim visited fellow musicians like [bassist] Rubão Sabino," Nelson Motta recounts.

> Along with Tibério Gaspar, Rubão rented a house in Recreio dos Bandeirantes [western suburb of Rio de Janeiro], in a beautiful area with wild beaches and even more deserted and remote than Barra da Tijuca. With Paulinho and Dafé in a white Chevette, Tim visited frequently, enjoying the solitude of Recreio and the company of the homeowners. He would take some mescaline, talking about flying saucers with Tibério and playing music with Rubão.[1]

Tim was done with acid following a disastrous televised performance where his tripping bandmates missed the show entirely. From then on "he carried a small bottle of organic mescaline, which had no amphetamines and did not have the connections with acid, only soft and colorful little trips."[2] But rather than let Nelson tell the story, let's hear from someone who was actually there, Tibério Gaspar:

Mine and Tim's friendship was really great. I used to live in Recreio dos Bandeirantes and Tim would go there all the time. One day he showed up in the morning and I was about to take a shower, so I told him, "come in, I'm gonna take a shower." He came in to my living room and I went to the bathroom. And I had this book, the Rational Culture book [*Universe in Disenchantment*], because the Rational Culture book is an interesting thing.

My father was a fantastic mathematician, very cultured, spoke various languages, he was a scholarly professor of biomathematics, celestial mechanics, physics and mathematics. He corresponded with some of the greatest scientists in the world. And he got involved in this. He went to the house of this Manoel Jacintho Coelho and he saw the most interesting thing. He came back and told me, "I met this guy, this Black guy, and I couldn't believe it, he had the idea of quantum philosophy all in his head. He intuited it. This is an incredible thing." My father even wrote the preface to the book [only in the rare, yellow first edition of *Universe in Disenchantment*]. It was this book that was on top of my table in the living room and Tim went in there and grabbed it.

And so, when I got out of the bathroom Tim asked me about the book and I told him that a colleague of my father's, a geologist, took my father to meet this guy, Seu Manoel who wrote that book. Manoel lived in a Moroccan style house in Belford Roxo. He holds his meetings there, he plays guitar, he's a musician. He made some incredible predictions. He predicted twenty years into my future.[3] How could he do that? He really had these powers. So, when Tim asked to go, I took him.[4]

While Tibério returned to Belford Roxo a few times after his father first took him there, compelled by the endless esoteric

Figure 6 *The original first edition, vol. 1 of 3 of the original (yellow) volumes with Tibério's father's preface. Courtesy of Paulinho Guitarra.*

explorations, samba jam sessions, and possibly the many young, female devotees, he never actually joined the sect. About Seu Manoel, "I agreed. I thought he was an amazing person. He was an entirely empirical guy who had many experiences in his life and understood everything. And he had a spiritual side that was very strong. He was a sorcerer, a wizard. Incredible!"

At first glance, Tim's attraction to Rational Culture was a complete shock to his friends and family. Later in life he went on record saying, "Religion [is] the cancer of mankind."[5] By all accounts from those I interviewed, Tim Maia was never a fan of organized religions, especially not the Catholic faith that he was raised in and to which his dear mother was devoted. "Tim's mom was very Catholic, his whole family was very Catholic," Tibério Gaspar explains.

> "Dona Imaculada," just imagine, your mom's name is "Immaculate." She was very religious. I got to know her. All of his siblings were raised this way. They were a poor family but very strict and proper. His father owned a boarding house and passed away at an early age. They were very polite, everybody very honest, but the black sheep was always Tim Maia.

Paulinho Guitarra seconds this notion: "His family was very religious, big into Jesus, and he didn't like it. He didn't like how his mom was always praying for help."

It's only fitting that it was UFO elements of the Rational Culture pitch that initially captured Tim's attention. A self-proclaimed UFO nut,[6] imagine you're Tim chancing upon this book with an intriguing image on the cover of a giant arch illuminated by rays of light shining down on a mass of people, one of them considerably larger than the others. There's also a large skeleton key with the words: "The key to the door of your salvation is in your hands." You're high on mescaline, waiting for your friend to get out of the shower, how are you not going to open this incredible book? Having read much of the first volume myself, I can vouch that the book wastes no time getting into the alien stuff, unlike Scientology texts, which only get interesting after you've spent hundreds of thousands of dollars on metaphysical audits.

"I got into this thing because I took some mescaline. I popped fifty of them. Then I was tripping my ass off and in the middle of the trip I said: 'Oh, I'll turn to Jesus, Ave Maria' (laughing) . . . that's how I got into this," Tim said, hopefully exaggerating the number of pills popped pre-revelation, but something in the book captured Tim's imagination. "I got into it because of ufology, I have been to several symposiums, I try to meet people who are interested in extraterrestrials. . . . I have never had contact, but I know of cases, I always study them. So, I went to this sect, which promised to prepare me for contact with extraterrestrials," Tim told Ruy Castro in 1991.[7]

Two days after chancing upon the book, Tim called his guitarist and second-in-command, Paulinho Guitarra, to talk to him about something extremely important. "Tim called me. 'Paulinho, you like flying saucers, right? You gotta come over here and check out this book that Tibério Gaspar showed me,'" Paulinho Guitarra remembers.

> I went there. I went to Tim's place every day. "Check out this book that Tibério lent me. It talks about everything, the origin of mankind . . . ." He was clearly excited. I couldn't believe that Tim Maia would believe in something like this . . . . He was serious. We made a plan. Tim, Tibério and me went to Belford Roxo to the Rational Culture headquarters.

Nowadays it only takes forty-five minutes to travel from Copacabana to Belford Roxo, a northern satellite city of Rio de Janeiro, thanks to the new freeway, but back in 1974 it took at least twice as long. Tim, Tibério, and Paulinho arrived late in the evening in Tim's little, white Chevette. Nelson Motta sets the scene: "The house was old and modest, with dark and heavy furniture. Next to it was a shed with a tin-roof that was transformed into a small auditorium with wooden benches, where the faithful read the book, became immune and improved their lives."[8]

Then there was the man of the house: Manoel Jacintho Coelho a.k.a. Seu Manoel. Again, Nelson Motta: "Manoel Jacintho Coelho was a light-skinned mulatto, strong and wiry, who did not look his seventy years and he was six and a half feet tall. Dressed all in white, as awe inspiring as an *Umbanda* priest, his figure and his booming voice demanded respect, even from Tim Maia."[9] Paulinho picks up the story:

> Manoel Jacintho Coelho was a mystic. When he smoked his *charuto* [a Brazilian cigar] his eyes would get all crazy, like a mad man. . . . We left at five o'clock or six o'clock. The sun was just coming up. We left with the shirts, books and promotional materials. Tim was convinced, "flying saucers are real . . . now we know where we came from . . . ."

By my account, Tim discovered Tibério's copy of *Universe in Disenchantment* around March or April 1974 with Tim, Tibério, and Paulinho's trip to Belford Roxo taking place shortly thereafter. I don't mean to belabor the exactitude of when Tim joined and left Rational Culture, but there's been a good deal of public confusion about how long Tim actually had been involved with Rational Culture. For example, Motta's book has Tim discovering the book a few months later, in August 1974.

I consulted Don Pi, who was only eighteen years old at the time, so it's understandable if the timeline is a little blurry forty years later. "Everything happened so quickly; there was a lot going on." Pi recalls things started to change while he was still traveling back and forth nearly weekly between Barra Mansa (during the week in order to finish high school) and Rio de Janeiro (on the weekends either playing gigs with Tim's band or participating in rehearsals or recording sessions). As a result of his weekly absence, he's not sure exactly when Tim first encountered the *Universe in Disenchantment* book, but he's certain it was before he finished school and returned to Rio in June, because he remembers already receiving a book from Tim on a previous weekend visit.

With the approximate start date established, Don Pi confirms that the final show where Tim Maia performed as a member of Rational Culture was a show in Passa Quatro in the state of Minas Gerais in late September 1975. By this accounting, Tim Maia actively participated in Rational Culture for about seventeen months, from around May 1974 until late September 1975. We'll get into the details of his conversion shortly, but it's worth noting, by looking at photos from these early months (May–October) that Tim didn't embrace all aspects of Rational Culture immediately, in terms of dressing only in white, shaving his facial hair and cutting his afro as we can see from this photo from October 1974.

Contrary to the existing narrative, it appears Tim eased into Rational Culture for the first few months, at least in terms of his wardrobe. Rare footage exists of Tim's performance at the Grand Opening of the Bandeirantes Theater in São Paulo on August 12, 1974, the first time he played one of his new songs after playing some of his big hits from his last album, "Réu Confesso" (I Confess), "Primavera" (Spring), and "Azul Da Cor Do Mar" (Blue the Color of the Sea), to the cheers of the thousands of attendees. Dressed in what appears to be a

Figure 7 *Banda da Seroma Racional, October 6, 1974. Left to right: Tim Maia, Paulinho Guitarra, Paulinho Martins, Robério Raphael, Robson Jorge, Beto Cajueiro, and Serginho Trombone. From the archive of Paulinho Guitarra.*

navy, crushed velvet blazer over a pink collared shirt, below his smiling and semi-bearded face (mutton chops that almost reach his chin), Tim's bubbling with energy onstage, grooving and adlibbing constantly, keeping the Seroma band on their toes. Tim introduces his band (including "the boss" Paulinho Guitarra and "Jorge Robson" on keyboards) before introducing the next song, "Que Beleza" (What A Beauty), which was the first time he ever spoke publicly about Rational Culture, a few months after he'd started reading the book: "The next song that we're gonna do here is about a book that I'm reading that I think all of you should read, called *Universe in Disenchantment* about rational immunization . . . [to the band] let's bring it!"[10]

By December 1974, Tim appears in photos dressed only in white and concert performances from that time show the band members also dressed in white, like Figure 8 showing Tim, Paulinho, and Carlos Dafé at a show in Irajá, a northern suburb of Rio de Janeiro. "Hey, Paulinho, look at the sky, do you see that?" Paulinho remembers Tim asking, but it wasn't flying saucers Tim was looking for, "it's Rational energy, it looks like smoke in the sky. . . . He was looking for energy [in the sky] without the help of smoking [marijuana]." Sure, on the surface it sounds crazy to follow your bandleader into an esoteric adventure starring a towering mulatto clairvoyant who believed in extraterrestrials and better living through demagnetization, but Tim Maia believed it and his excitement was contagious. "The general impression of myself and others in the band was, 'damn, Tim Maia doesn't believe in anything and now he's into this book,

Figure 8 *Tim Maia Racional concert, Irajá, Rio de Janeiro. Left to right: Paulinho Guitarra, Tim Maia, and Carlos Dafé. Archive of Paulinho Guitarra.*

so at the very least let's check it out and maybe we'll learn something new,'" Paulinho Guitarra remembers thinking. The band was re-baptized as the Banda Seroma Racional (Seroma Rational Band) with the choice put to all of Tim's musicians: join Rational Culture or leave the band. "We went with him and a large part of the band joined," Paulinho Guitarra said.

"Our lives before that were really pretty crazy," Paulinho Trompete #1 (de Oliveira) says,

and since Tim was like our leader in this crazy scene, when he went to this thing we went with him, we changed into the white shirts too. It was good for me to stop those crazy things and to lead a more correct life. We could see the fruits it gave us, each one giving the other confidence to pursue this new life. It was really good for us.

Building off the clubhouse vibe Tim fostered at their endless Seroma rehearsals, Tim and his bandmates' camaraderie extended beyond the RCA recording sessions, says Paulinho Trompete #1: "We were really united, we'd go to the beach and evangelize in 40 degrees [Celsius = 104 Fahrenheit] all dressed in white, handing out pamphlets." Just imagine, Tim and band finish a marathon recording session in Botafogo and then hit the streets or Copacabana beach to hand out pamphlets and spread the word about Rational Culture to anyone and everyone, like if James Brown donned Hare Krishna robes and took the J.B.'s down to Times Square to gain some converts!

Even the band's instruments were painted white, upon Seu Manoel's recommendation, due to the negative magnetism caused by the horn sections' metallic shine. "Tim had to buy two cans of white enamel paint and along with the musicians, they painted all the instruments, even the saxophones, trumpets and trombone, and the only thing that escaped a coat of paint were the piano's black keys," Nelson Motta jokes. "Although not a special paint, perhaps a miracle of Superior Rational, the sound of the instruments was not affected."[11]

Whether the band members were convinced by the doctrine or by the professional obligations as one of Tim Maia's musicians, few (if any) band members opted out entirely. Some musicians, like Oberdan Magalhães, Robson Jorge, and Serginho Trombone, were increasingly in demand around Rio's recording studios and night clubs, but even they suited up in the required white Racional-emblazoned T-shirt, white pants, and white shoes for gigs if Tim asked them and their schedules allowed it.

Out there and loving his new Rational Culture life, Tim made sure his musical apostles were towing the Rational line. "In the studio, he checked to see which musicians had read the book. Some leafed through it, others lied, but nobody understood anything," Nelson Motta asserts in his book. But again, Paulinho stresses that, at least in the beginning, most of the band was all-in, abstaining from drugs, at least. Contradicting another popular myth about Tim's Rational phase, at least for the band members "beer and cachaça [were fine], just no drugs . . . joints, cocaine, L.S.D., mescaline, no, but alcohol? Whatever. Cigarettes [were also fine]." Asking Paulinho if Tim regularly policed his bandmates for narcotics violations, he said, "No, no, because the musicians believed in Rational Culture [too]. 'Let's get clean, man, yeah, let's stay clean!' I didn't need Tim to [say anything] . . . everyone was straight, no drugs for five months." Five months.

Figure 9 *Left to right: Paulo Cesar Batera, Valdecir Nei Machado, Agenor Mendes Filho, Paulinho Guitarra. Photo courtesy of Paulinho Guitarra.*

Tim's tour of Rational duty was almost a year and a half, meaning most of the band didn't stick with Rational Culture nearly as long as he did.

Sometime between May and December 1974—I'm guessing somewhere around November—Tim Maia went full Rational, dressing only in white, eating differently, abstaining from drugs and alcohol and reading the book non-stop. For the first time since leaving his mother's house in 1959, Tim was eating healthily. "He was not smoking grass, so he did not have that appetite for [red] meat," Pi recalls. "He was not eating cow and pork meat. He would sometimes eat fish. He was very disciplined about these things, because everything that was red was for the devil!" Looking at a photo of Tim from this phase, he's still a big man and certainly would be classified as overweight, but his appearance is noticeably slimmer. His torso is stuffed into a too-small T-shirt, his hair is cropped short, and his face is clean-shaven for the first time in likely a decade. The pictures of Tim during his Rational phase are a reminder that underneath the soul crooner's awesome afro and rock star attire, Tim looked just like many anonymous, overweight Afro-Brazilians. Paulinho remembers that:

> it was 1974 when we recorded all the backing tracks. We had already started recording the song "Que Beleza" and the lyrics had been already approved [by the censor] before the Rational thing happened.[12] It was completed when he was already reading [the book], but he didn't want to refer to it explicitly, "Que beleza . . . a natureza" [What a beauty . . . the nature], but it didn't refer directly to the book. It was the only one.

All of the bandmates I interviewed confirmed that most of the songs they were working on for the RCA double album had scratch vocals, stand-in lyrics that Tim would sing that may or may not have materialized into the final lyrics. Paulinho Guitarra remembers, "He put some guide lyrics [on these songs] when he was composing them, singing lyrics over various melodies in the studio and lots of things were ready, that people don't know about, before he started to read this book." By all accounts, this process began during the summer of 1974, maybe June, July, or August. "All of a sudden he says, 'we're gonna turn the whole thing around,' but what he meant was only the lyrics," Don Pi remembers. "He decided to erase them, to throw them into the garbage and record different lyrics from the book," Paulinho said, visibly still sad that Tim's original secular versions were lost in the process. "It's a shame that those original lyrics to these songs don't exist [anymore]."

Tim was eager to impress his new guru, so "once he recorded the first new lyrics, Tim was running to take the tapes to Seu Manoel Jacintho," Nelson Motta writes.

> The master loved them, and there was a feeling of great potential for the promotion of the group, which re-encouraged Tim to be more explicit in his songs about Rational Culture, talking about the book and its teachings. The immunization process required total dedication, it was necessary to free the material world and make his music an instrument of the will of the Superior Rational.

Motta continues:

> The apartment on Figueiredo de Magalhães was empty. Tim had donated everything, including the stove and refrigerator, leaving only a mattress. He took his sound equipment to Belford Roxo and donated it all to the Rational Superior. He was a holy man dedicated to sowing good, an ascetic in search of purity and enlightenment by rational immunization to deliver him from his animality and his magnetism and take him back to his home planet on a ship piloted by Manoel Jacintho.[13]

I believe Tim knew that he was into something controversial, something that might make the label nervous. I theorize that he consciously (or subconsciously) tried to keep his new lyrical intentions under wraps for as long as possible, delaying the inevitable confrontation so that he could continue using the

Botafogo studios free of charge, finishing as much of his double album as possible before the RCA executives could catch on. That could also explain why "Que Beleza" is the only song mentioned in these early months and it's the only song that doesn't make explicit reference to Rational Culture. The song served as a shot across the bow and as predicted, RCA wanted to have a word with Tim. "They [RCA] were panicked because they had a two-album contract in writing with Tim, the advance money was already paid, and so they panicked when they heard of what kind of music he was now making, who's gonna buy this shit?" Don Pi remembers.

There's debate about how exactly Tim ended up walking away from his RCA deal with the master tapes of the nearly complete double album. Nelson Motta's book asserts that Seu Manoel provided the money for Tim to buy the tapes, but given how much Tim had recently donated, wasn't that just Tim's money anyways? In an interview in *Playboy* magazine in 1991 Tim supported this version, referring to Seu Manoel: "He was also smart and bought ten reels of tape that I had recorded on RCA. With these tapes we made two LPs and four singles."[14] Don Pi balks at this idea: "Seu Manoel didn't put any money into this project." A version of dubious truthiness, but with a certain Tim Maia quality to it, tells of Tim and band storming the studios and stealing the tapes, all dressed in white and making a scene, like a Hare Krishna heist. "That's not true," Don Pi insists, but it certainly makes for an entertaining alternative history. If I had made the *Tim Maia* biopic and was playing fast and loose with facts, I would certainly film this scene!

Given Tim's multi-album contract with RCA, likely the record executives' worst fear was that Tim would actually hold them to the contract and insist on them releasing the two albums as Tim intended, Rational Culture lyrics and all. When pressured to do something he didn't want to do, Tim typically responded negatively and loudly, but Don Pi couldn't have been more surprised by Tim's response when the RCA executives confronted him:

> I remember that Tim's reaction was very special, because they were expecting that he would explode, because he always did that when someone tried to put a thing on his music. He wouldn't accept that at all. At that time, surprisingly, he reacted cool. Because when they came to him in the studio to tell him, "hey, we cannot sell this, man. You know, your fans will not understand this, and we cannot sell this. How can we release something like that?" Then Tim said, "here's the deal, give me the tapes. Give the tapes to me and we'll just cancel the contract," and everybody was like [look of shock] . . . . They were ready for war, you know? But that never happened. He was just, "alright, this is what I'm gonna do, I don't give a shit, I have the money!"

Cancel the contract, give Tim the tapes, and forget about the nearly $300,000 in advance money (that was quickly making its way from Tim's wallet to Rational Culture's coffers), that's all the RCA executives had to do. You can't blame them; the real expense in making records comes after the music's recorded and you have to master, design, press and promote, distribute, and market the album. When RCA signed Tim Maia, they thought they bought the goose that laid the golden egg and then all they got from Tim were two new age propaganda albums; it was a case of right musician, wrong time. Tim Maia never released an iota of music on RCA, but they managed to bankroll a majority of his double album and paid him the better part of a half-million (back in the early 1970s!); now, who's the crazy one?

Before diving into the songs on these two albums, there's a theory that has led some critics and fans to come to the conclusion that the Rational albums are so great, in part, because Tim and band were sober during their Rational Culture phase. However, when it comes to the music itself, the instrumental backing tracks, all of the songs from *Racional* Vol. 1 and *Racional* Vol. 2 were finalized (or close to completion) at the RCA studios between January and April/May 1974, prior to Tim's conversion. As was normal at any pre-Rational recording sessions, marijuana smoke wafted like incense and LSD sparked creative compositions through extended jam sessions. Paulinho Guitarra confirms that at the same time, Tim and the band were still toking heavily: "A lot . . . all day, every day!" Tim was sober, however, when he recorded the new Rational vocals at Somil, an independent studio close to Tim's apartment in Copacabana, after liberating the backing tracks from RCA. Listening to the vocals on his Rational albums, it's clear that Tim was stretching out vocally, never sounding better than he did on these recordings. "He looks so skinny and his voice was so powerful," Paulinho Guitarra remembers.

Interlude: Searching for Light during Brazil's Dark Years

You have from the mid-sixties, this kind of unraveling of conventional social modes, you have psychedelics entering in and rewriting people's minds, all of the political tensions of the time lead to this explosive Dionysian energy . . . leads to a lot of very puzzled, very confused, very lost people and when you hit the early seventies and indeed things are starting to spiral down the toilet, people start searching big time which is why so many people turned to intense forms of religious and spiritual practice.

ERIK DAVIS, *THE SOURCE FAMILY*[1]

During the darkest years of the Brazil's military dictatorship, his experience was really not that unique given what was going on. Tim wasn't the only Brazilian looking to the stars or deep into a mystical book to make sense of the world around them where a brutal US-backed military regime held their country captive.

During the late 1960s and early 1970s, many of the same schisms and tensions that fueled domestic foment in the United States were also evident in Brazil, such as counterculture youth movements, the increasing influence of pop culture, increased immigration and introduction of foreign ideas and philosophies. "During the hardest period of the military dictatorship, now known as the 'dark years,' many people embarked upon esotericism as a way to escape the reigning square attitude," read the liner-notes from the recent Brazilian reissue of *Tim Maia Racional* Vol. 1:

> Usually such incursions, relatively common among artists, saw drugs as a gateway or propellant. Raul Seixas and his then partner, Paulo Coelho [author of international best-seller, *The Alchemist*], created the Alternative Society as a lysergic and anarchist panacea, based on the teachings of the British occultist Aleister Crowley. Several books with mystical appeal became best sellers in Brazil. Many people followed *The Morning of the Magicians*, a discourse by French researchers Louis Pauwels and Jacques Bergier. *The Teachings of Don Juan* [known in Brazil as: *The Devil's Herb*], by writer and Spanish American anthropologist Carlos Castaneda, in which he recounts his experiences under the influence of mescaline, captured the imagination of many Brazilians. Titles by the polemical writer Lobsang Rampa, such as *The Third Vision*, *The Monks of Tibet* and *The Cave of the Ancients*, which explored the mystical dimension of Tibetan Buddhism, filled the shelves of bookstores with their flashy covers and the heads of readers with expressions like "astral travel" and "transmigration." The magazine *Planeta*, dedicated to esoteric topics, was then one of the best-selling publications in Brazil.[2]

Beginning in the late 1960s and gaining steam in the early 1970s around the time Tim joined, Rational Culture found purchase with a new generation of Brazilians in search of meaning. It also benefited from having a charismatic and, according to some, prophetic leader in Seu Manoel. "Most new religions emerge within a previously existing religious context, a context which initially nurtured it and from which it draws basic insights," Christopher Partridge writes in *New Religions: A Guide*.

> However, a minority of new religions have developed as the products of innovative women and men and present themselves as genuinely new phenomena even after the roots of their teachings have been explored. Such is the case with many groups born from the teachings of a new prophet: The Nation of Islam, The Meher Baba Movement, Yiguandao and the Church of Scientology.

The book, *Universe in Disenchantment*, Rational Culture legend tells, was transcribed to paper through telepathic messages received by Seu Manoel from the all-powerful entity that is responsible for Rational Culture: The Superior Rational. When Seu Manoel initially became disenchanted in 1935, space and other cosmic frontiers were not exactly household topics, but by the 1970s a new generation of baby-boomer Brazilians were primed for Seu Manoel's far-out vision. Tim Maia was one of Seu Manoel's most avid disciples for about eighteen months from 1974 to 1975, but he certainly wasn't the only celebrity or musician hanging out at Seu Manoel's Belford Roxo compound.

Not unlike the Church of Scientology, Rational Culture attracted celebrities, particularly musicians. In addition to Jackson do Pandeiro, who's something like a Little Richard in terms of his bedrock importance in Brazilian popular music, Rational Culture also attracted the legendary samba composer João Roberto Kelly and Luperce Miranda, one of the country's greatest mandolin players. Nelson Motta recounts that Seu Manoel

> really liked samba and sometimes hosted a jam session in his backyard where excited devotees sang lyrics about Rational Culture. With trembling fingers showing the early signs of Parkinsons, the master could no longer play [guitar], but he loved singing accompanied by Tim's guitar, Jackson's tambourine and the mandolin of Luperce, one of the greatest trios in the history of Brazilian music in praise of Rational Culture.[3]

Some celebrities dipped a toe in, checked it out, but didn't go all-in like Jackson, João Roberto, and Tim. Paulinho Trompete #1 (Paulo Roberto de Oliveira) remembers Jorge Ben Jor's brief flirtation with Rational Culture, even meeting with Seu Manoel at Belford Roxo. "Even Jorge Ben was there for a bit," Paulinho Trompete #1 recalls, "but I think he saw that we weren't making any money and he left before too long." The beloved variety TV show host Chacrinha (imagine the lovechild of Johnny Carson and Captain Kangaroo) even visited with Seu Manoel on occasion. Both Carloses, Roberto and Erasmo, read the book, at least one volume. Like Jorge Ben Jor, Erasmo, and Roberto, many of the new celebrity guests visiting Seu Manoel at the Belford Roxo compound came at Tim's invitation, and usually at his insistence.

Whether Seu Manoel intentionally sought out celebrities as a means of recruiting the public through the resulting publicity or because he genuinely enjoyed and felt validated by his celebrity connections, we'll never know for sure, but we do know that despite being black, Seu Manoel experienced a very privileged position in Rio de Janeiro society. "His job, as civil servant at the Foreign Ministry, can also explain a possible key to his readings and influences," Neumann explains. "His official status set him apart from the anonymous masses. [Seu Manoel's status] raised him to a privileged position, both for his relatively comfortable financial status, or perhaps, the wide range of contacts in his day-to-day."[4] His unique standing in Rio de Janeiro society, straddling the white world of government and the black world of Afro-Brazilian spiritualism, allowed him to rub shoulders with all spectrums of society. "In his biography Coelho never tired of telling his biographer the countless meetings with celebrities of politics and music. Coelho's 'contacts' ranged from [President] Vargas to [iconic samba composer] Cartola."[5]

Figure 10 *Left to right: Unknown singer, Tim Maia on bass in background, Geraldo on drums in foreground with cigarette, Tibério Gaspar with long hair mixing the sound, Paulinho Guitarra, unknown percussion player. Belford Roxo, 1975. Photo courtesy of Paulinho Guitarra.*

Tim likely felt he was in good company amidst the other notable musicians in the mix. "There were other artists like Jackson do Pandeiro and even Procopio Ferreira, poor man, before his death, [he] was a part of the fad of Universe in Disenchantment," Tim said in an interview. "It was really crazy . . . Lucio Mauro, a bit of an artist, you know? Altamiro Carrilho . . . . Everyone was in the game."[6] Tim went on to record no fewer than two full albums and most of a third, all proselytizing the word of Rational Culture and at the same time João Roberto Kelly, Jackson do Pandeiro, and Altamiro Carrilho all released records within a year of Tim's Rational records yet none of them were dedicated to Rational Culture. After Tim, Jackson do Pandeiro was the only major artist that recorded and released a few songs about Rational Culture across two of his 1970s albums.[7] Perhaps learning a tough business lesson from Tim Maia, he never released a full album singing the praises of Rational Culture. But that was Tim Maia. If he was excited about anything, he went for it 110 percent, bringing his band and entourage with him.

4 *Tim Maia Racional* Vol. 1 (Late 1974)

Tim had already launched Seroma Productions, his production company in 1973 at Tibério Gaspar's suggestion. "Make your own publishing company, brother," Tibério remembers telling Tim and now that he needed his own label to release his new recordings on, he doubled down on Seroma. "'It will be your label,' I told him, 'like all of the musicians in the U.S. have.'" True, at least two of Tim's North American musician idols established their own publishing companies and record labels just a few years earlier: Curtis Mayfield started Curtom and the Isely Brothers launched T-Neck. In Tim's classic do-it-yourself style, he asked Paulinho Guitarra for help: "[imitating Tim] 'Let's start our record label, Seroma. Paulinho you studied art, make a logo for our label!'" True, Paulinho studied fine arts, in addition to rock and soul, while in high school and still enjoys painting and drawing. Of the sketched logos Paulinho uncovered in his mementos there's one's made of smoke (wink, wink) and another features Tim's beloved German Shepherds Tula and Tila (idea credited to a Flávio), but eventually Tim settled on something more iconic. The eventual logo, chosen while Tim was already deep in Rational Culture, reflected his new obsession. "We saw it in *Planeta*, a magazine about UFO things," Paulinho Guitarra remembers, referring to the squat oval shape they chose to encircle the name, "Seroma." "In the photo, the UFO is elliptical and that's why the final logo is an ellipse with 'Seroma' written inside."

A quick note about the musicians who played on both *Racional* Vol. 1 and 2: Since Seroma wasn't the most organized business venture, the records of who played on what tracks simply do not exist; however, Paulinho Guitarra kept his own personal notes (or he may have been the unofficial Seroma scribe) about these sessions. These two albums in particular, likely because they were being recorded over a long period of time on RCA's dime, called on the skills of a large number of musicians with no one person playing the same instrument on every track, with the possible exception of Paulinho Guitarra

Figure 11 *Early sketches for Tim's record label, Seroma. Drawings courtesy of Paulinho Guitarra.*

Figure 12 *Early sketches for Tim's record label, Seroma. Drawings courtesy of Paulinho Guitarra.*

on lead guitar and Tim on lead vocals. According to Paulinho Guitarra's memory and notes, twenty-four people put their stamp on the tracks that became *Tim Maia Racional* Vol. 1 and *Tim Maia Racional* Vol. 2, and that doesn't even include Don Pi, who was in and out of the band at that time, having just joined and going back and forth to Barra Mansa to finish school. Don Pi has memories of rehearsals from this time, but he's not certain he played on sessions for the album, almost all of which were recorded at RCA's Botafogo studio.

Drums: Roberio Rafael, Paulinho Batera, and Luiz Carlos Fuina

Bass: Beto Cajueiro, Robson Jorge, Tim Maia, and Paulinho Guitarra

Guitars: Paulinho Guitarra, Robson Jorge, Cassiano, Tim Maia, Ari Piazzarolo, Beto Cajueiro

12-string guitar: Neco

Keyboards (Fender Rhodes, Wurltizer, Honher Clavinet, Hammond organ): Robson Jorge, Sergingho Trombone, and Don Charles

Percussion: Luiz Carlos Fuina, Hermes, Ariovaldo, Ronaldo, Chacal, and Chaplin

Horns: Serginho Trombone (trombone), Paulinho de Oliveira and Paulinho Martins (trumpets), Oberdan Magalhães (saxes and flute), and Tim Maia (flute)

Additional players:
Back-up vocals: Amaro and Camarão (Os Diagonais)
Guitar and vocals: Fábio
Hammond organ and Fender Rhodes: José Roberto Bertrami

With the new Rational vocals recorded, an LP cover was designed based on existing Rational Culture iconography and by the end of 1974 Tim Maia became the most successful and famous Brazilian musician, before or since, to independently release his own record, *Tim Maia Racional* Vol. 1. The first song that anyone likely heard of Tim's Rational recordings back in the 1970s, or during the album's revival decades later, was "Que Beleza." It was released on a single and was the only song distributed (by hand) to local radio stations. At least a year since his previous release in 1973, "Que Beleza" with its opaque references to Rational Culture stood a chance of becoming a hit and even received nominal radio airplay in Rio de Janeiro in early 1975. Decades later, the song helped stoke interest in Tim's long-forgotten Rational albums, thanks to cover versions by Gal Costa and Marisa Monte.

"Immunização Racional (Que Beleza)" opens *Tim Maia Racional* Vol. 1 ominously with a moody flute melody (played by Tim) over Beto Cajueiro's rolling bass line. Paulinho Guitarra's slinky guitar jags in and out with slippery licks and wah-wah strokes while Don Pi's piano keeps the song from sinking too deeply into the funk with his insistent, uplifting comping. All the while, the drummer keeps time submerged in a profoundly deep pocket, understated, yet funky as hell. The song makes no mention of "Rational Culture" explicitly, though he peppers the song's mystical and righteous lyrics with references to "disenchantment," "purity," and "knowing your past and your future." The most explicit reference to Rational Culture is in the title itself, "Immunização Racional (Que Beleza)," though most everyone knows the song by its parenthetical title and sing-along chorus. As if to alert the listener that this was not your usual Tim Maia release, "Que Beleza" opens the album in a haunting, even a little foreboding mood, with minor-key chords creating a cognitive dissonance with Tim's triumphant lyrics delivered so passionately.

The album continues like a radio show, with introductions before some songs, such as the second song, "O Grão Mestre Varonil," the title, an obscure reference to Seu Manoel (The Manly Grandmaster) sung a cappella. After speaking the song's title, Tim spends the next twenty seconds singing Seu Manoel's praises as "The greatest man in the world" and a "missionary of purity." Musically, the ditty resembles a short Christian hymn, a song format Tim was certainly familiar as an altar boy growing up in a strict Catholic household. As the album's third song is about to start, it's certainly clear to any listener that this is a unique record.

The short descending notes that Tim sings at the end of his Rational hymn to Seu Manoel perfectly set up the listener for the album's third song, "Bom Senso," which emerges from the pregnant silence to casual strums of an electric bass and tentative electric guitar jangles that create a melancholic and introspective musical mood. Lyrically, "Bom Senso" is one of Tim's greatest compositions, drawing from some of his own tragic life experiences to explain his embrace of Rational Culture. Tim proselytizes to potential converts with the zeal of someone recently born again. For the first thirty seconds Tim delivers a proto-rap, sounding like Saul Williams slamming some def poetry, verbally speeding up from the last song's a cappella "walk" to a lyrical "jog" as the drummer joins in (twenty-seconds deep) as Tim sings:

> Já senti saudade (I've felt the blues)
> Já fiz muita coisa errada (I've done many things wrong)
> Já pedi ajuda (I've asked for help)
> Já dormi na rua (I've slept in the streets)

Cascading brass, courtesy of Oberdan Magalhães, Serginho Trombone, and both the Paulinho Trompetes, soaring strings and Serginho Trombone's percussive clavinet jolt the listener out of the song's delicious depression, introducing musical and existential salvation with the words sung twice, "but reading I reached the common sense." What is the "common sense," you ask? "The Rational Immunization," Tim sings after a dramatic pause as Paulinho Guitarra's snarling guitar punctuates these words, sung syllable-by-syllable with his Ernie Isely–inspired be-phasered slashes. Paulinho's jagged chords float for a few seconds, descending and then disappearing as Tim repeats the dark, autobiographical intro verses. Once again, the horns, strings, funky keyboard, and searing guitar return to remind the listener about the book being the portal to achieving "common sense." As the song winds down, Tim insists over a simmering groove, "to not waste any time, read the book *Universe in Disenchantment.*"

Another a cappella interlude follows, titled "Energia Racional" (Rational Energy), which Tim sings in a bizarre style, sounding something like a cross between a preacher and a boxing announcer. "I had to climb, up there on high, to see" (Eu tive que subir, lá no alto, para ver), Tim shouts dramatically, pausing before he sings the final words in a noticeably more relaxed tone, "Rational energy, the true light of humanity" (Energia racional a verdadeira luz da humanidade).

None of the bandmates could remember any of the scratch lyrics for these songs from *Racional* Vol. 1, barring the first version of "Que Beleza," with its pre-Rational lyrics, but I think it's a fair bet that the next song, "Leio O Livro Universo Em Desencanto" was a love song. This is the first song (of many) from the Rational recordings where Tim and the band experimented using different foundational texts found in *Universe in Disenchantment* after jettisoning Tim's original secular lyrics. With its couples' dance tempo and lilting strings, this tender tune is a classic, saccharine slow jam if not for the strangely explicit mantra-like lyrics:

Leia o livro (Read the book)

Universo em Desencanto (Universe in Disenchantment)

Leia o livro (Read the book)

Universo em Desencanto (Universe in Disenchantment)

Leia e vai saber o que é encanto (Read and you will know what is enchantment)

Leia e vai salvar o desencanto (Read and you will be saved from disenchantment)

The next song, "Contato com o Mundo Racional" (Contact with the Rational World) similarly repeats the same four lines over a mellow groove built around acoustic guitar, electric bass, drums, and Tim's pleading vocals, begging for "just one contact" (resta apenas um contato) with the Rational World, where "you will see beauty beyond equal" (vôce vai ver beleza sem igual). This song shows Tim blurring the lines between the spiritual and the sensual. Musically, "Contato Com O Mundo Racional" oozes late-night yearning, while the lyrics speak of spiritual searching, a dichotomy Tim exploits more than once during his turbulent Seroma years, most notably on his first post-Racional single, "Ela Partiu," where Tim's lyrics lament a lost lover, while the intensity of the music and delivery suggest a more existential loss.

Perhaps the weakest song, musically, is *Racional* Vol. 1's most lyrically informative song. Cherry-picking phrases from the book *Universe in Disenchantment*, the song "Universo em Desencanto" explains the origins of humanity over a jaunty, samba-soul groove, like how man and woman were born of "resin and gum." Similar to "Bom Senso," Tim uses a change of key, to minor-chords to introduce humanity's "disease" that can only be cured by the book. Around the song's half-way point, Tim slows the tempo to a bossa nova shuffle laced with a solitary violin and delicate electric guitar licks and sing-talks about getting, "in touch with our pure, clean and perfect brothers," sung over the band's outro groove before slowly fading out.

"Que Beleza" may be the best-known song from Tim's Rational recordings, but the double-whammy of "You Don't Know What I Know" and the twelve-plus minute funk opus "Rational Culture"—both sung entirely in English—are the most iconic and mind-blowing. With "You Don't Know What I Know," Tim perfected his Rational hymn stylistically and with this captivating thirty-second vocal performance. Tim sings, "You don't know what I know, because I know where we came from. We came from a super world, [a] world of Rational energy, and we live in a[n] anti-world, [a] world of animal's energy. Read the book, the only book, the book of God, *Universe in Disenchantment*, and you're gonna know the true." As soon as Tim sings his final word, "true," the stankiest funk groove this side of Isaac Hayes emerges from the pregnant silence. Built on an almost excruciatingly slow beat (ninety-two beats-per-minute) layered with at least three keyboards (playful clavinet, comping Fender Rhodes, and churchy Hammond organ), insistent electric bass, handclaps, Paulinho completes the instrumental with his double-tracked guitars, one plucking funky figures while another blows fuzzy smoke-rings through the murky mess, that is, until Tim's voice emerges two minutes and twenty-four seconds into the marathon groove, singing, "We gonna rule the world, don't you know, don't you know? We gonna put it together."

Tim's English-language entry had the potential to do more than energize dancefloors or facilitate love-making, as he evangelized to his North American brothers over a vamping clavinet and Paulinho's extended phaser-ific guitar solos. Nearly ten minutes deep, following one of the many joyous group rejoinders ("gonna put it together"), Tim goes into his sing-talk mode, stressing, in English, "so, listen, once more, don't forget, read the book, the only book, the book of God, *Universe in Disenchantment*, don't waste your time, don't waste your time, read the book, *Universe in Disenchantment*, and you're gonna know the true," as Tim's Rational chorus repeats, "gonna put it together," over and over to a relentless, religious funk vamp. I can only imagine the reaction of your casual Tim Maia fan who managed to listen to *Tim Maia Racional* Vol. 1 when it was released in late 1974: confused, excited, confused, dancing, and then left with a spinning head after digesting the most epic funk jam to ever grace Brazilian wax with the album's final song, "Rational Culture."

Certainly, *Racional* Vol. 1 was no average Brazilian pop album, independently released as it was, but a twelve-minute song was unheard of for a Brazilian release, barring classical or folkloric records. More than anything, "Rational Culture" is a showcase for Tim's Seroma band. Luiz Carlos Fuina's funky drumming combined with band handclaps and an ever-present tambourine, layered with keyboards and Paulinho's diverse guitar work make an otherwise repetitive funk vamp nearly transcendent. Sometimes Tim used the Rational Culture text to entrance listeners, stimulating a possible conversion, and sometimes he used music, coaxing funk-friendly listeners to follow the groove, like an existential pied-piper to Seu Manoel's doorstep in Belford Roxo.

Tim Maia Racional Vol. 1 clocks in at thirty-four minutes, split between nine songs, three of them Tim's a cappella Rational hymns. "Que Beleza" and "Bom Senso," two of the three best-known and most-loved tunes from the album surpass the five-minute mark, while "Rational Culture" breaks every rule in pop music, clocking in at well over ten minutes. Tim completed the album, finalized the arrangements, recording the Rational vocals and the a cappella Rational hymns, mixing the album and even designing the labels, covers, and insert after parting ways with RCA, leaving him to make all the final decisions about sequencing, mixing, editing, and so forth. For an album recorded by a popular musician in a popular style (Brazilian soul, funk, and pop), *Racional* Vol. 1 breaks a couple of the most basic rules with songs too long to play on the radio, not to mention the bizarre cover art.

"When music is separated from its commercial reasons then it has this other thing about it," says Yale Evelev, president of Luaka Bop Records, the New York-based record label that released the first compilation of Tim Maia's music for non-Brazilian audiences, which included no fewer than six songs from the two Rational records. "The Rational stuff was not there to be sold, you're not making songs to be played on the radio and that's a freeing thing that allows someone to make something they wouldn't have made otherwise, especially someone who always worked in a commercial realm, and it gives another quality to the music." From the music, to the album's marketing and distribution, to the album art, Tim Maia's Rational recordings confused and delighted in equal measure.

The covers for *Racional* Vol. 1 and 2 are nearly identical save that on *Racional* Vol. 2 the "Vol. 2" appears below in the same large blue font: "Tim Maia Racional." For *Racional* Vol. 1, the "Vol.

Figure 13 *Cover of* Tim Maia Racional *Vol. 1.*

1" appears in the same place, but in black and almost comically small, like where's-the-magnifying-glass small. Given Rational Culture's obsession with reading, it only makes sense that the album covers would be full of text.

Looking like a Dr. Bronner's Soap label with a few more pictures, the texts annotate the images, helping to explain Rational Culture to whomever might pick up the album. The largest image is of a bright sun shining across a moon-and-star-dotted-sky as it moves from day to night over a mountainous landscape. The words "Mundo Racional" (Rational World) in red are the largest on the cover aside from "Tim Maia Racional." In the upper left corner, there's something like a legend, that reads: "This map shows us the transformation of the deformed electric and magnetic energy for your natural state that is clean, Rational energy, pure and perfect." To the right of the sun-moon-stars image is the same image that appears on the cover of *Universe in Disenchantment*, depicting an ornate arch emanating light upon masses of black-and-white people with one large person towering over the rest. Above the arch appear four ellipses, the same gold color as the arch, getting progressively smaller as they stretch from the arch upward. The image is titled "Porta do Mundo Racional" (Door to the Rational World). Below these two larger images is a series of smaller images, arranged like a comic-strip with arrows instructing the reader to move from left to right. The first one shows a suited man with the words "The cause of being human is the microbe." The next image looks like the contents of a particularly festive petri dish with the annotation "The cause of the microbe is the body of rational energy." The third image is of the same floating gold ellipse from above the arch with the words "The cause of the body of rational energy is the rational world, because there is no effect without cause." Still with me? The next arrow leads us to even more text: "For it's inside rational culture that a person acquires the rational light, the body of rational energy, that is here inside this deformation. Return to your world of origin the rational world, for you are illuminated by the rational light." There's yet another arrow and even more text, that makes less sense than the first four diagrams.

Everything that appears on the cover of the album, all the images and text, were copied directly from existing Rational Culture propaganda, mostly the book, except for a couple sentences that appear at the beginning and end of a small paragraph in the bottom right corner under the sub-title: "Connecting everyone to their world of origin." The paragraph starts, "The words of the rational songs are connected to Rational Energy, the pure energy, clean and perfect, because it's of the Superworld. . . . So, my gentlemen! Buy the records of Rational Energy that eliminate the evils of the body, and the evils of life."

5 Rational Friends and Family (Early 1975)

Zooming back for a moment from the rapid and radical changes going on in Tim's life, it becomes clear that Tim's brief flirtation with a higher order also coincides with his brief attempt at a "normal" domestic life with a partner, kids, dogs, and so on. Tim's domestic dream became reality while Tim, Geisa, and the gang were neck-deep in Rational Culture on January 24, 1975, when Geisa gave birth to Tim's own son, Carmelo Maia . . . or was it Telmo Maia? Before the child was born, Tim asked Seu Manoel what to name his child to ensure he grew up happy and rationally immunized. Nelson Motta writes in *Vale Tudo*:

> "Robson, Telmo or Carmelo," responded the Superior Rational through the mouth of Coelho, but between Belford Roxo and the Civil Registry in Copacabana, Tim hesitated between Telmo and Carmelo. Robson was likely eliminated given Tim's existing confusion around keyboard player Robson Jorge's name. He registered the baby's name as Carmelo, however when he returned to the house, he announced: "the name of the kid is Telmo," it was Manoel Jacintho that recommended it.[1]

This discrepancy went completely unnoticed until Telmo started attending school and his teachers concluded the boy was deaf when he failed to respond to repeated announcements of "Carmelo" during roll call. For a brief period of time, a couple months, Tim and family almost resembled a normal, Brazilian family, that is, minus the Rational Culture stuff. "I was pretty square. I even had a child because I was so detoxed,"[2] Tim said in his interview with *Playboy* magazine.

"Baby Telmo and Leo, now one year old, both having been demagnetized by Manoel and, like his father and mother, wearing only white and instead of lullabies, they listened to their father read them the book," Motta writes. From a 2007 documentary about Tim's life, Léo Maia recalls that "according to Rational Culture, toys are things of the devil, so he threw away all of my toys, leaving me nothing!"[3] Sadly, Tim's strange version of domestic bliss was short lived. Geisa, probably suffering from post-partum depression (maybe the same reason she left Campos the first time), booked it again for Campos with Léo, leaving baby Telmo with Tim and Pi. "Tim and I had to take care of the boy," Pi remembers, "so, I was the one taking care of the boy, because Tim was too busy to do that. He was a baby [about changing diapers, etc.]." Like an unholy mash-up of *Three Men and a Baby*, *The Making Of a Band*, and *Ancient Aliens*, Don Pi and Tim Maia found themselves caring for an infant, while sinking deeper and deeper into the Rational Culture universe.

Within weeks of being left alone at home with baby Telmo, Tim's mother, Dona Imaculada, came to the Copacabana apartment with one of Tim's sisters, Anna Maria, and very calmly dressed the baby, packing his things as if they were taking him to the beach as they sometimes did. But they didn't return, taking Telmo with them back to Tijuca and raising him in a way that Tim and Pi could not. "Carmelo was raised like a prince and we didn't have the condition to do that," Pi explained, relieved, as he was the one changing the diapers, buying the baby food, and waking when the boy cried in the middle of the night. Pi remembers that Tim liked to read to Telmo from *Universe in Disenchantment*, play him some guitar and sing to him, but beyond that it was all Pi. Nonetheless, Tim was heartbroken, and wept when he'd realized what his mother had done.

Don Pi recalls that Tim was heartbroken for a few days without baby Telmo around, but with all of the Rational Culture activity and plans to release the second volume of his Rational recordings, he didn't mope around the apartment for long. Early 1975 found Tim at his deepest in the Rational Culture world, attending conferences about UFOs, regular Rational Culture lectures, epic conversations with Seu Manoel, and demagnetized jam sessions at Rational Culture headquarters. Tim even rented an apartment across the street from the Rational Culture compound in Belford Roxo, where Don Pi also lived for much of 1975 with Tim. Asking Tibério Gaspar why he thought Tim committed so intensely to Rational Culture, more than himself or the other musicians they knew, he says:

> I think he went deep. He went further. . . . It was his own idea to make a record talking about Rational Culture. He was making propaganda for the book. Seu Manoel approved and since he no longer had a record company he could use the followers to sell the albums. "Let's go sell the records!" It became a very local success, because the albums didn't enter the discos, they didn't play on the radio, it was a hidden thing because it wasn't in record stores, only in and around Rio de Janeiro.

Figure 14 *Manoel Jacintho Coelho (smoking on left) and Paulinho Guitarra (second from right), all others unknown. Photo courtesy of Paulinho Guitarra.*

Rational Culture was a process to go through before becoming fully demagnetized and rationally immunized. In Tim's typical style, he charged ahead at full speed, determined to reach rational immunization as quickly as possible. In 1975, on the verge of releasing the second volume of Rational recordings, Tim went on an evangelizing spree, making the media stops, all the talk shows and variety shows. Beyond that, Tim and his Rational Culture entourage would often press the flesh with the good people of Rio de Janeiro. "All in white T-shirts with the logo of Rational [Culture], Tim and his musicians roamed the downtown streets of Copacabana playing, singing and preaching Rational Culture, selling records and books at the newsstands and on the sidewalk and to drivers waiting at red lights," Nelson Motta writes.[4]

"Tim Maia is sitting on a stool all dressed in white; his 115-kilo [254-pound] mass doesn't allow his pants to fasten. His t-shirt has the design of a portal illuminated by a column of rays of light coming from above and the phrase 'Cultura Racional,'" goes the opening sentence of an article from the January 1975 edition of *Pop* magazine, a Brazilian entertainment tabloid. "Tim Maia Is Now a Guru" is the title with the words "He wants to save humanity" in a pop-out bubble. The article continues, "Around him, sitting on the floor, also dressed in white and wearing the same t-shirt, are the members of his new group: The Seroma Racional Band: Paulinho [Guitarra], Serginho [Trombone], Betinho Cajueiro and Roberto [Rafael]. Everyone is reading the same book." After ten minutes Tim closes his book, takes a deep breath and looks over to the reporter writing this article and calls out: "Hey, magnetic!" to let the outsider know he was ready to talk:

> And with that the really bizarre chat with the 32-year-old, fat singer began. Surprisingly, Tim goes on to say he does not want anything to do with spiritualism: "Spiritualism is an enigma that everyone dreams that they have, but they've never proven it, and they never will prove it. I'm looking to raise myself up through Rational Culture."

Tibério clarifies this point, saying that Tim really didn't see Rational Culture as a religion, and part of its appeal for Tim was that it didn't call itself a religion or spiritual community. "He was totally against these ideas. He fanatically hated sects," Tibério says. The main reason that Rational Culture separates itself from other traditional or new religions is because their bible, their body of wisdom, "*Universe in Disenchantment*, wasn't written, it was dictated by the Rational Superior in the voice of Manoel Jacintho Coelho."[5] According to Rational Culture followers, this is fact, not some apostles, or some guy named Mohamed, remembering what happened to the best of their ability.

Tim also didn't appreciate any comparisons to other "spiritual" escapes, like Brazilian rocker Raul Seixas who founded the "Alternative Society" with lyricist and all-time best-selling Portuguese language author, Paulo Coelho. "John Lennon is a beast, and Raul Seixas is a Xerox copy of the same bullshit. They are two quadrupeds who just want justification for enjoying that madness. It's an insane trick!"[6]

Within a matter of months, Tim's Seroma clubhouse and Copacabana apartment went from the bustling nerve centers of Brazil's soul music scene with countless friends and guests coming and going, dozens of dogs, booze, and party favors aplenty, to drug-free centers for Seroma Rational Band meetings and rehearsals. Some musicians were momentarily out of Tim's orbit when his lifestyle suddenly changed. One such musician, pianist and singer Carlos Dafé, came by Tim's apartment one day looking to smoke a joint and jam. Instead, he found Tim's apartment bustling with people all dressed in white. Immediately, Tim put a book in Dafé's hands as well as a T-shirt, white pants and white shoes.

When Tim heard what Dafé was up to, singing and playing piano at the stuffy Hotel Nacional in downtown Rio de Janeiro, he immediately convinced his new convert to advance the cause. "Sell those books there in the hotel," Tim insisted, "then come back here I'll take you to meet the man. And read the book!" Nelson Motta explains what happened next: "The management at the Hotel Nacional did not like to see that little, Black pianist all dressed in white with a strange logo on his shirt, offering these weird books. Dafé was forced to put back on his magnetic clothes and disown his faith in order to not lose his job."[7]

Tim's closest friends outside of the band, like Hyldon, Tibério Gaspar, and Erasmo Carlos, no longer knew how to act around their old friend in his white clothes always talking about this strange book. Some friends and acquaintances gave Tim the benefit of the doubt and even tried to read the book. Tim's old friend Hyldon was riding high at this point, one of the rising stars of the Soul Brasileiro scene, having launched his solo career the year before with the iconic single, "Na Rua, Na Chuva, Na Fazenda" (In the Street, In the Rain, On the Farm) and a fantastic full-length from early 1975. As one of Tim's closest friends and favorite musicians, Hyldon often stopped by Seroma studios to jam with Tim or rehearse songs. In 1975, he was working on songs for his second album, *Deus, a Natureza e a Música* (God, Nature and Music) (Polydor, 1976).

Tim, when he entered into the Rational thing, it was all of a sudden. I found out when he came by my house. I was living in São Conrado and he would come by often to go to the beach or just to hang out. There was nothing there, a desert at that time, no asphalt, only dirt roads. And he gave me a book as a present. He was dressed in white saying, "man, you gotta check out this book. This book is going to change your life. It's connected to this group Rational Culture."

So, I started to read the book. By the third or fourth page I said, "I'm not gonna read this anymore. I don't believe anything written in this book, this foolishness." Later he passed by the house and shouted up to me, "How is it? Are you reading the book, my man?" I lied, "Hey Tim, I'm on page 46." And then some time passes, maybe fifteen days and he asked me, "You read it already, right?" "I'm reading it, man." "What page are you on?" "I'm on page 46 . . . ." He became boring as hell, singing like a motherfucker on those records that I think are really great, but I don't like the lyrics.

Even after receiving the cold shoulder from his old friend Erasmo from back in the Tijuca days, Tim and he later reconciled, though the same can't be said for Tim and Roberto. "Nothing from him ever surprised me," Erasmo recounts in his autobiography, *Meu Fama De Mau,* about his old friend Tim. "In 1975, he sent me a copy of the book *Universe in Disenchantment* with the dedication:

> Mr. Erasmo Carlos:
>
> Even someone as discredited and carefree as yourself will be immunized. All you have to do is read and reread the book *Universe in Disenchantment: The Origin of Mankind.* Read it carefully and do not judge it until you have finished reading the whole book.
>
> Rational Tim Maia, before crazy, now straight"[8]

Tibério Gaspar has a different perspective as someone who believed Seu Manoel to be a unique individual and capable of prophesies and possessing an intellect and knowledge of everything from science, to music, to politics to herbal healing. "I joined, but not to the degree that Tim did, because Tim became fanatical," Tibério explains. "Tim is just that way. I don't like fanaticism. I don't like any kind of fanaticism." Tibério was curious, but he drew the line when Tim urged him to be more committed to Rational Culture: "I told him, 'look, man, I'm not gonna do that, because I'm not gonna dive into any sect or religion all the way. I think it's incredible and cool, I'll go there, I love it there [Belford Roxo], but I'm not going to join any sect and become a member of anything. I didn't want to be a follower of anything.'"

Eduardo Araújo observed mostly from a distance, always maintaining his home base in São Paulo. "He called me, we talked all the time, about everything. In reality, I was like a quasi-guru for him," Eduardo says. "When he told me [he had joined Rational Culture], on the one hand, I thought it was a good thing because he'd quit all the drugs and made a marvelous record." Like Tim's other musician friends, Eduardo received books and copies of the records and knowing that Tim made them, of course he listened to them, and being able to listen past the bizarre lyrics, he heard the fantastic music therein, possibly his best yet. "People don't remember this," Eduardo insists, "but he was at the height of his success and when the record company didn't want to put out his record and he started his independent label, the final record was really good despite not having a proper record label overseeing everything."

Another Afro-Brazilian from Rio de Janeiro that got his start under Carlos Imperial's guidance was Wilson Simonal, but that's about where his similarities with Tim end. Simonal was more Jackie Wilson to Tim's James Brown, but just like those two American entertainers, Tim and Wilson shared a great rapport and evidently Tim got Wilson hooked on the books. After getting caught up in a serious game of political tag, Simonal was mistakenly labeled as a military informant, a charge from which his career never fully recovered.[9] "When, in November 1974, Simonal was sentenced to prison by the military justice system that said he was an informant, at least he had the forethought to listen to his condemnatory sentence while carrying a copy of *Universe in Disenchantment* in his hands," Pedro Alexandre Sanches writes in his investigation of *Jovem Guarda* and M.P.B. pop stars in his book *Como Dois E Dois São Cinco: Roberto Carlos (& Erasmo & Wanderléa)*. "He got the book from Tim Maia."[10]

Tim wasn't the only Afro-Brazilian music star seeking solace in esoteric ideas. "The extraterrestrials who are already arriving, 'our pure, clean and perfect brothers,' were first cousins of the alchemists, 'discreet and silent,' 'patient, assiduous and persevering,' as Jorge Ben Jor's in "Os Alquimistas Estão Chegando," writes Pedro Alexandre Sanches:

> Even the graphic design of the 1974 albums of Tim's and Ben's were similar looking, but if Tim Maia was looking to the sky watching for extraterrestrial saviors, Jorge leaned in his own way on the holy philosopher St. Thomas Aquinas and his medieval alchemists. The pressure was too much for M.P.B. to bear. They buried the poor censors in a cascade of original music, waterfalls of insane text, looking at the extraterrestrial sky and the medieval earth just so as to not have to look their own dictatorship in the face.[11]

Tim's recruitment efforts did not stop at the Brazilian border. Tim announced that he sent copies of the book, in Portuguese, to James Brown, Curtis Mayfield, and John Lennon, convinced that

Figure 15 *Jorge Ben Jor's album* A Tábua De Esmeralda *(Philips Records, 1974).*

"the Superior Rational is made so that anyone can understand." Not necessarily so, it would seem, as Tim received a response from John Lennon: a photo of the ex-Beatle, entirely nude, with a note—"Dear freak, I don't understand Portuguese. What about LISTEN to this photo? John Lennon."[12]

Closer to home, Tim's large family, just over in Tijuca, couldn't escape his evangelical duties urging them all to read the book. The family offered a solid show of support, buying the book, going to the concerts and buying the albums, but there were no conversions as they were all staunch Catholics. One of the unanticipated silver linings to Tim's conversion and extreme interpretation of Rational Culture doctrine was that he gave away most of his personal belongings, of which his entire record collection ended up with Tim's sister, Ed Motta's mom.

Ed Motta, a global underground star of experimental jazz, funk, and pop, is also Tim's nephew, which has not always been an enviable title. Ed has great love for his uncle and a deep respect for his music, but like anything with family, things can get complicated.

> I was very young [four years old]. I remember some things. I remember when he turned to the Rational religion [laughs] and it was strong and he used to give to the whole family T-shirts and things related to that and he gave to my mother his complete record collection because he didn't want to have anything material, so that's how I got into contact with Sly Stone, Curtis Mayfield, The Drifters, Rance Allen Group, Isley Brothers, they were his influences, Charles Wright, these sorts of things.

Keep in mind that most of these records were imported and not readily available to the average kindergartener, as his uncle's influence and his inheritance of these records may have something to do with Ed Motta's precocious beginnings: signing to a major label at sixteen years old, playing a mixture of R&B, funk, soul, and pop music. "It was for me a very important period because at a very early age I found out that music was the thing that I was supposed to do, was more than a pleasure, was something really magical, like all the time. Because I used to be there with my parents playing instruments and listening to albums."

As a musician himself, who considers his uncle one of his formative influences, the Rational recordings are special in his uncle's catalog:

> I remember for me when I was young, it was one of my favorites, *Racional Vol. 1* and the cover art was very important to me because I was into Earth, Wind & Fire and things, and I used to see a connection between that kinda spacy, kinda Sun Ra cover art. For me it was very important, and I never had Volume 2 and I still don't have it 'til this day.

Which says something about the rarity of Volume 2 given Ed's reputation as one of Brazil's premier and persnicketiest record collectors. "It's pretty expensive to find in mint condition."[13]

For the bandmates that really had no choice but to join Tim in this Rational Culture thing or leave the band, some really did believe, like Tim did, while others just played along. Looking back on these times with a bit of hindsight, it's easy to recast one's experience on the side of "playing along" with Tim's newest obsession as Paulinho Guitarra seems to do in some moments during our interview, while in another, he says, "I believed in the book, so I read it. . . . It was inside of us, we didn't need anyone telling us to read [the book]. I was reading because I wanted to reach 'Rational Immunization!'" In response to the assertion in both Nelson Motta and Fábio's books about band members being required to read a certain number of pages before rehearsal, Paulinho says, "No, the truth is that everyone had to read always! Not just before rehearsals, always . . . and we went there [to Belford Roxo] every week, [where] we listened to lectures. Every week there would be a day when we would go there, and someone would read a passage from the book." Looking at a photo of Tim and Paulinho in a large conference room surrounded by others in white, Paulinho explains: "At the time of Rational Culture, we took part in many seminars and conferences about Ufology and this photo shows us at one of these things, Tim and me, I think in São Paulo."

Don Pi, on the other hand, claims that he never believed in Rational Culture, but faked it to stay a part of Tim's world:

I used to go to the beach and sometimes I liked to smoke some joints, but it was absolutely forbidden. He would look at your eyes; he would smell your hands and look at you really closely. To fool that man with that much [drug] experience, would be nearly impossible. But my trick was to go to Copacabana beach and jump in the ocean with the salt water and afterwards your eyes are gonna be red anyways, so I used to go with my joint there, do a little swimming, put some eye drops in my eyes and before going back to the house I would pass by Gordon's, which was like a McDonald's or Burger King, and I'd call up to the apartment from the pay phone in front asking if he wanted anything. And when I brought the food, he wouldn't pay attention to my eyes, he would only pay attention to the food!

It was really funny, because all of a sudden it was not so easy to hang around with Tim reading this book all the time. The music was great. The atmosphere was great, it was the best, I think, the second-best phase of his career as a singer and also as a person. He became very, very gentle and became very calm. He was very, I would say, "rational." [laughs] He was very sweet too, very generous. But the thing is, to read the book and buy the book all the time—and you could not lend your book to someone else—and it was not one or two or three books, it was nine books and they were not cheap. But I was just pretending that I was reading. Look, I was his maid, I was his friend and I was doing everything around the house: buying food, going to the pharmacy, going shopping, taking care of his finances, going downtown and I was pretty much busy with all these things, so I didn't have a lot of freedom or time.

Being a member of the Tim Maia band was always a full-time job, but before Tim became involved with Rational Culture, that job mostly consisted of doing drugs and jamming; now they had additional Rational duties. "We, the band, and Tim Maia used to go out in the neighborhoods knocking door to door, 'Hello, ma'am, I'm Tim Maia. I want to show you this book, the salvation of all humanity, about the history of humanity. . . .'" Paulinho Guitarra regurgitates his old spiel. According to Paulinho's memory, Tim and band canvassed most of Niterói and large chunks of urban Rio in about a year's time. But then he had some help: "The only advantage was that I had twenty-two neurotic fanatics saluting me. They sold my records in [all over] Brazil and come back with the accounts just right, and then they say 'amen.' Fanatics are great for sales."

Fanatics might be great for sales, but they were a liability when it came to Tim's public concerts, which were fewer and fewer as promoters came to learn about Tim's new "show" and the 100-plus guest list of Rational Culture groupies he demanded enter for free, severely cutting any profits. There were also some Rational Culture sponsored shows by and for the followers of Rational Culture, where attendees sought rational demagnetization through Tim and his band's music.

6 *Tim Maia Racional* Vol. 2 (Early–Mid 1975)

Tim Maia Racional Vol. 1, the very first release on Tim's Seroma label as "Seroma-001," was released in late 1974 as was the related EP (Seroma 0003), containing "Immunização Racional (Que Beleza)," "Universo Em Desencanto," as well as edited versions of "Rational Culture" and "Bom Senso." Tim's do-it-yourself business approach meant that *Racional* Vol. 1 slowly trickled out to into the world, sold door-to-door by Rational Culture followers, and on consignment in dozens of independent record stores throughout Rio de Janeiro. Caught up in the excitement and eager to reach Rational nirvana, Tim got back to work in early 1975, putting the finishing touches on the remaining tracks from his planned double album for RCA.

"In 1975, he finalized a few backing tracks we'd recorded that didn't have lyrics yet, never had lyrics," Paulinho Guitarra remembers of the album that would become *Racional* Vol. 2. Paulinho confirms that the main difference, if any, between *Racional* Vol. 1 and *Racional* Vol. 2 is that the songs that ended up on the first album all had non-Rational lyrics before Tim recorded over them. *Racional* Vol. 2 includes some songs that previously had non-Rational Culture lyrics, mostly written by bandmates or Tim's friends. At least one song, "O Caminho Do Bem," came together, music and lyrics, during the brief window when Tim and band were fully immersed in Rational Culture, and still recording at the RCA studios in Botafogo. With an album's worth of top-shelf instrumental funk on tape, Tim wasted little time getting back into the studio, going back to the nearby independent studio, Somil, to finish the second record of his now serialized double album.

The other notable difference between the two volumes is that while every song on *Racional* Vol. 1 was credited to "Tim Maia Racional," songs written by Tim's band members and friends dominated *Racional* Vol. 2. In some cases, the song Tim received included finished lyrics about topics unrelated to Rational Culture, so Tim kept the music and completely rewrote the lyrics in praise of Rational Culture and Seu Manoel.

The one song that Paulinho Guitarra, Don Pi, and Eduardo Araújo all remembered that received this treatment is the first song from *Racional* Vol. 2, the monster Latin funk song originally written by Tim's friend, singer, and songwriter Fábio. "Fábio was a good friend of Tim's. Tim adored Fábio and he was there every day, with Tim at his house, and one day he showed him this song and he recorded it," Paulinho Guitarra recalls. The song was originally called "Adios San Juan del Puerto Rico," and it was about "going to San Juan and meeting a girl, you know how these things go, that was the theme of the whole thing," Pi remembers, but once Tim was done with it, it became "Quer Queira, Quer Não Queira" (Whether You Like It or Not). Paulinho even remembered the song's original first line, singing "Yo nasci em San Juan del Puerto Rico . . . ."

"Quer Queira, Quer Não Queira" kicks off *Racional* Vol. 2 with a jolt built around Beto Cajueiro's monster bass line that pushes Robério Raphael's percolating funk beat accented by Agenor

Mendes Filho's percussion, Paulinho's wah-wahing strokes, and Robson Jorge's bubbling Hammond B-3 organ stabs. Tim's urgent vocals hijack the groove around the thirty-seconds mark, insisting confidently that "like it or not, everyone's gonna read *Universe in Disenchantment*, that has messages from a superior place. What's needed is really simple: read and re-read," with the band joining in with powerful vocal harmonies as Tim sings, "re-ler" (re-read). The song goes off-script from the go-to Rational Culture texts, riffing on themes over an incendiary rhythm track, once again pierced with a nasty, Isely Brothers–worthy guitar solo courtesy of electric guitar *wunderkind*, Paulinho Guitarra.

As if to allow the listener a rest-lap, the next song, "Paz Interior" (Internal Peace), bounces along to a more relaxed samba-soul tempo not dissimilar from "Gostava Tanto de Você" from Tim's 1973 album, which makes sense, as it was also written by Tim's old bandmate from the Os Tijucanos do Ritmo and the Snakes, Edson Trindade. Curiously, there's no other composer credited on this song, meaning Edson wrote the lyrics as well, making it safe to assume Tim got his old buddy from Tijuca drinking the Rational Kool-Aid too! One can only imagine, given the proper sentimental lyrics and Tim's romantic delivery, how a secular version of "Paz Interior" might have dominated the Brazilian pop charts in early 1975, just like "Gostava Tanto de Você" did in 1973. The song's bouncing samba beat and uplifting horns mirror the song's positive message, lyrically similar to "Que Beleza" as Edson writes about Rational Culture's benefits only mentioning the word "Rational" once in the song's middle verse:

Voltou o brilho dos meus olhos (The brightness of my eyes returned)

Voltou a paz interior (The inner peace returned)

No universo em desencanto (In the disenchanted universe)

Que reencontrei com muito amor (That I found again with much love)

Racional (Rational)

"O Caminho Do Bem" (The Good Path), is likely the second-best-known song from the Rational recordings after "Que Beleza," mostly due of its prominent placement during the closing credits of the 2002 Brazilian film that received widespread international distribution, *Cidade De Deus* (City of God). As the film's narrator proudly concludes that he survived the drug-trafficking world of his *favela* home to become a professional journalist, "O Caminho do Bem" plays in the background, lyrically complimenting the narrator's message, while the song's somber and pensive mood doesn't let the viewer forget the film's darkness and violence. According to Paulinho Guitarra, the song emerged from a jam session back at the RCA studios:

> "O Caminho Do Bem" was a groove we created in the studio with Serginho Trombone on the clavinet and Beto Cajueiro trying to fit Rational prose to [that groove]. It was a transcription, basically, from the chapter of the book called "O Caminho Do Bem." Beto started repeating the words "O Caminho Do Bem" over a certain part in the groove … even Tim helped Beto [with the lyrics to the song]. The basic tracks were recorded before, and the lyrics were added after. There never existed non-Rational lyrics for this song.

The song is a unique one in Tim's catalog with its slow-as-molasses funk beat and Tim's almost-whispered vocals sounding almost like a musical mantra meant to accompany a religious ritual or an outtake from Lee Perry's Black Ark studios. Beto's bass and Serginho's clavinet drive the song along while Paulinho's guitar snakes in and out as a cow bell punctuates the proceedings, sounding like an insistent rattlesnake. Musically, the song resembles an Isely Brothers slow jam with Tim's vocals suggesting the tenderness of Ronnie Isely's vocal delivery while the rhythm track keeps things fresh with soulful Fender Rhodes licks and Paulinho's scorching guitar (free of phaser-effect) taking the song to its six-plus-minute conclusion.

"Energia Racional" carries the same name and takes direct inspiration from a track with the same title from *Racional* Vol. 1. Remember this twelve-second Rational hymn: "I had to climb, up there on high, to see . . . Rational energy, the true light of humanity?" Kicking off with a tight burst of a drum break, this tune from *Racional* Vol. 2 finds Tim singing the same phrase over a rhythmically intense instrumental track built around another perfectly synched bass and drum combo and brimming with congas, acoustic and electric guitars, clavinet, piano and organ, and what sounds like muted trombone. The band stretches out over an almost three-minute funk trance while Tim repeats the above mantra about Rational energy. At this point, you're either dancing and having a Rational revelation, or dancing and chuckling to yourself about the absurdity of it all.

Latin influences appear on the Rational recordings more than any recordings of Tim's, which is best explained by a couple of his North American influences around that time, namely, Santana and the Isely Brothers, who were not a Latin group in any way, but often employed congas and borrowed some Latin rhythms. "Que Legal" (How Cool) even more than "Quer Queira Quer Não

Queira," flaunts Latin instrumentation with prominent timbales, congas, and a classic piano line from the Cuban tradition that makes the song sound like a salsa-samba-funk hybrid. Written by Tim Maia Racional, as the title of the song hints, this is where Tim gets real and speaks directly to the sceptics and possible converts in his down-to-earth lyrics in defense of Rational Culture:

> É legal, (It's cool)
>
> a cultura viva racional (the rational living culture)
>
> É bacana (It's cool)
>
> mas tem muita gente que se engana (but there are many people who are mistaken)
>
> Pensam mal (They think it's bad)
>
> mas é cultura vinda pra o bem (but it is a culture coming for good)
>
> do Brasil (of Brazil)
>
> e você vai ter que ler também (and you'll have to read it too)

About a minute into this pulsing track, Tim goes on to explain in his Rational preacher style that Rational Culture is not a religion, sect, doctrine, science, philosophy, spiritualism, or knowledge, going on to explain that Rational Culture "comes from our true world of origin, it did not originate from any human mind, it was dictated by the Superior Rational," referring to the Rational Culture's incorporeal God, if they believed in deities. Tim sings the first verse again before sharing some more Rational facts over funky beats. A gurgling clavinet counterpoints the Caribbean Fender Rhodes groove played with occasional, tasteful string accents drifting in before Paulinho brings the song to a final climax with a guitar solo that owes more to Carlos Santana than Ernie Isely.

"At that time, whoever read more books would be closer to seeing the Rational Light," Paulinho Trompete #1 remembers thinking. "I was on the third or fourth book, but Paulinho Guitarra was way ahead." It's said that among Tim's band, Paulinho Guitarra and Beto Cajueiro went the deepest and most enthusiastically into Rational Culture. The band's bassist, Beto Cajueiro, and his wife, Ana Cristina Lins Cajueiro, were also said to have committed intensely to Rational Culture and Seu Manoel. In addition to helping to compose the music and fit the Rational text to "O Caminho Do Bem," Beto also composed "Cultura Racional," with only the Superior Rational providing guidance. It's another Rational ballad, similar in its sentimentality to "Leio O Livro Universo Em Desencanto" from the previous album. Over a lilting piano and acoustic-guitar-accented instrumental track, Tim croons:

> Saia depressa (Get out quickly)
>
> Desta fogueira infernal (From this infernal fire)
>
> E vá habitar o seu mundo (And go and inhabit your world)
>
> Que é natural (Which is natural)

Robson Jorge, the pianist, multi-instrumentalist, and future producer to Brazil's stars, composed "O Dever De Fazer Propaganda Deste Conhecimento" (The Duty to Propagate This Knowledge), lyrics and everything. Following an incongruous string-laden introduction, pierced with a couple of fuzzy guitar strums, the song unfolds over a lazy beat that employs much of the same instrumentation as the previous track, emotive strings and all. Clocking in at nearly six minutes, the best part comes in the final forty-five seconds as Tim playfully scats over a mellow outro groove.

The final new song on *Racional* Vol. 1 is a delight with a bizarre title, "Guiné Bissau, Moçambique E Angola Racional," which answers the question on everyone's mind: what rhymes with "numa relax, numa tranquila, numa boa." Tim is credited with composing the song in its entirety, though the lyrics, again, are little more than a mantra:

Eu vim aqui para lhe dizer (I came here to tell you)

Eu vim aqui para lhe dizer (I came here to tell you)

Que eles agora estão (That they are now)

Numa relax (In a relaxed [mood])

Numa tranquila (In a quiet [mood])

Numa boa (In a good [mood])

Numa relax (In a relaxed [mood])

Numa tranquila (In a quiet [mood])

Numa boa (In a good [mood])

Lendo os livros da Cultura Racional (Reading the books of Rational Culture)

Guiné Bissau, Moçambique e Angola (Guinea Bissau, Mozambique and Angola)

Guiné Bissau, Moçambique e Angola (Guinea Bissau, Mozambique and Angola)

The song opens with a simple piano riff played over a pulsing rhythm section, congas, and electric guitar accents filling in the holes between the spacious, yet taut, drum and bass combination. As Tim gets to the line about reading the books, fuzz guitar and horns surge, dropping off on a dime after Tim sings, "cultura racional." Tim and band play with time on this song, starting and stopping the beat ever-so-subtly, a trick he'd employ to fantastic effect on later albums. Just when you think the song's over, Tim hesitates a millisecond longer before bringing the beat back. This song is also a precursor to songs like "Rodésia" (Rhodesia, the previous name for what is now Zimbabwe), as well as "Brother, Father, Sister, Mother," both from Tim's first official album after departing Rational Culture (*Tim Maia*, Polydor, 1976), with their references, however superficial, to independence struggles in some of Africa's former European colonies. In order to transform the secular first draft of the song into a final Rational song, it seems plausible that all Tim needed to do was simply swap a line for the one line that references Rational Culture.

Tim ends his radically transformed double album with the same song he starts it with, "Immunização Racional (Que Beleza)," this time in a shorter and faster version. Interestingly, the version that appears on *Racional* Vol. 2 is the same version that Tim and band played on August 1974 for the grand opening of the Bandeirantes Theater. This version, with its insistent brass salvos and double-time drum kit and conga beat, is the version Luaka Bop used to open their Tim Maia compilation, *World Psychedelic Classics 4: Nobody Can Live Forever: The Existential Soul of Tim Maia*. If the version of the song that starts *Racional* Vol. 1 is meant to intrigue, the version that closes *Racional* Vol. 2 is meant to motivate with its propulsive beat, rocking piano, and the epic dual that erupts between Paulinho's phasered guitar and both of the other Paulinhos' trumpets. I urge you to seek out the live footage of the performance from the Bandeirantes Theater to get a rare glimpse into a song from these recordings performed live.[1]

During the recording sessions for *Racional* Vol. 2 Tim was thoroughly committed to Rational Culture and not interested in hearing anyone's critiques, especially not from the Seroma Rational Band, but Paulinho Guitarra was beginning to have his doubts. "He invested, he bought the equipment that they had there [in Belford Roxo], Tim left all that stuff there, recording equipment … everything he earned went there," Paulinho Guitarra says. Don Pi was fed-up and decided to say something to Tim:

> Tim and I had a big discussion at our apartment because I was trying to open his mind about all that cult bullshit. That was the first time I had a confrontation with him saying that the cult would destroy his career, which happened. This conversation was just before we went to the studio for this recording session for *Racional* Vol. 2. Until that point, nobody had the courage or influence to tell him anything bad about that cult. People were afraid. But I didn't care—I had no fear of being fired, if that happened. Until that point I had an opportunity to see many things around us that didn't make me feel very confident about what the leader of the cult, Mr. Manoel Jacintho Coelho, was saying. It didn't make any sense to invest all of Tim's time and money. I mean, it took all of his money! He was the only one who's paying for everything: he'd pay for the band, the studio sessions, for the cult's concerts, the equipment, etc.

Tim Maia Racional Vol. 2 hit the streets in mid-1975, only a few months after the first volume, quite literally being sold door-to-door and person-to-person by Rational Culture followers. Due to its limited time in circulation before Tim disavowed Rational Culture, it's said that Volume 2 only sold 20,000 copies, whereas the first volume supposedly sold 38,000 copies, either of which would be fantastic numbers for Brazil's earliest independent release.[2] Even though Tim and the Rational Culture sales team were at a distinct disadvantage against the large record companies, the door-to-door sales of the record around Rio were so successful that, according to Tibério Gaspar,

> Tim started to take notice when it became clear that despite the lack of a professional distribution system and sales team, the sales made by the followers of Seu Manoel were actually much better than the sales previously reported to Tim by Polydor for his first albums. And that's when I told him, "I think you were getting robbed, man."

Tim later returned to recording for Brazil's major labels, just about every single one of them, including Som Livre, Atlantic, Odeon, Lança, Continental, RCA, and BMG, but his experience running his own label and distribution system certainly gave him a unique insight into the myriad ways a record label can screw over one of their artists. In 1982, Tim explained this to Tárik de Souza, who begins:

> After selling two-hundred and ten thousand [210,000] copies officially during his debut [years 1970–4]—he prefers to talk about six hundred thousand [600,000], because, "record labels get a big chunk of SNF sales."[3] Tim zigzagged up to eighteen thousand copies in '76, before going through virtually all of the major labels, ranging from one hundred thousand to thirty thousand copies sold. "If it was up to the labels, I'd be making peanuts this whole time."[4]

7 *Tim Maia Racional* Vol. 3 and the End of Rationality

In 2012, fifteen years after Tim Maia's death, a mysterious bonus disc was included in a fifteen-volume box set of Tim's albums put together by Abril Collections and released exclusively at Brazil's many newsstands: *Tim Maia Racional* Vol. 3. Rumor has it these recordings were made in the final months before Tim returned to irrationality. Still holding down Tim's band despite the departure of a number of core band members—like Carlos Dafé, Serginho Trombone, Robson Jorge, and Luiz Carlos Fuina—Paulinho Guitarra was the last man standing from Tim's original Seroma heyday. "For [*Tim Maia Racional*] *Volume 1 & 2*, almost everything was recorded in 1974," Paulinho attempts to clarify the chronology of the Rational recordings. "A couple of things were finished in 1975, but by *Tim Maia Racional* Vol. 3 the band had already changed, some people came, some people went, and Tim said, 'let's go record some new things.'"

The band was Paulinho Cesar do Couto (a.k.a. Paulinho Batera) on drums, Oberdan Magalhães on saxophone, Paulinho Martins (a.k.a. Paulinho Trompete #2) on trumpet, Valdecir Nei on bass, Paulinho Guitarra on guitar, Agenor Mendes Filho on percussion,

Figure 16 *Band members who recorded* Tim Maia Racional *Vol. 3, left to right: Oberdan Magalhães, Paulinho Trompete #2 (Paulinho Martins), Valdecir Nei Machado, Paulinho Guitarra, Agenor Mendes Filho, Paulo Cesar Batera (obscured). Photo courtesy of Paulinho Guitarra.*

Don Pi on keyboards,[1] and Elza and Terezinha (last names not known) singing backup vocals. It's a lot of new faces, and then Oberdan, who must have been free at the time to play some sessions for an old friend and mentor. Oberdan wore the white T-shirt, but he never made it a lifestyle; he was too busy founding Banda Black Rio. "It was around June or July of 1975," Paulinho Guitarra remembers, "and it was almost the end [of the Rational Culture involvement when] Tim had us record some songs. It was a lot of backing tracks, a demo. When Tim left [Rational Culture] he didn't pay for the tapes and left them at the studio, it was all over for him." More than twenty years later a studio engineer named William Luna Jr. would stumble upon this tape and shepherd it to its eventual release as *Tim Maia Racional* Vol. 3 in 2012. Chapter 11 of this book goes into much greater detail about this release, the musicians and music therein.

By the middle of 1975 even Don Pi and Paulinho Guitarra, who were still playing gigs and recording with Tim throughout 1975, had stopped reading the book, dressing in white (when not performing with Tim's band), and attending lectures at Belford Roxo. Most importantly, they'd picked up their old habits: "When we stopped smoking marijuana, all of the band, everybody got really bored," Paulinho Guitarra explains.

> "Come on, Tim, no smoking?" And he would say, "no, we must be clean, we must be good." Ah, poor Tim . . . and I was the last one before Tim to go back [to smoking marijuana] . . . I stayed with it for five months. Me and the whole band and then after a while it [Rational Culture] didn't do anything for me.

Tim's commitment to Rational Culture correlated directly to his financial health. As long as he could afford to not earn any money, or give the little he made to Seu Manoel, Tim was content with his day-to-day existence, but his band members didn't have the same financial security going into Rational Culture as he did. After a while it became a matter of survival for these musicians to get paid work to feed themselves and their families. Paulinho Trompete #1 (Paulo Roberto de Oliveira) and Serginho Trombone stuck it out with Tim until one day it just became too much with Tim scanning the sky for signs of the "Rational Light," which would indicate his Rational Immunization was starting to kick in. "Tim's looking up at the sky and swearing he's seeing the Rational Light, so I turned to Serginho Trombone

Figure 17 *May 13, 1975 performance at Belford Roxo Rational Culture Center. Photo courtesy of Paulinho Guitarra.*

and said, 'let's get out of here.' And that's when we started let it all hang out again."

Certainly, Tim could still count on the hundreds of devoted Rational Culture followers to show up to gigs, but it was getting harder and harder to find the best musicians to play with him. He was still "Tim Maia of Brazil," and so Paulinho Guitarra was able to fill the holes in the band with players he knew from Niterói. Ironically, some of Tim's highest profile gigs while representing Rational Culture took place in the final months of his participation in the esoteric movement, like the presentation at Belford Roxo (Figure 17), in the public square, on May 13, 1975, as part of the celebrations for Brazil's holiday commemorating the end of slavery. It was the first official appearance of the Seroma Rational Band, with all of their instruments painted white. "I remember I saw the Rational concert live with Paulinho [Guitarra] on guitar, everyone wearing white shirts and it was in a small institute called Instituto Da Educação (Institute of Education) in Tijuca, my neighborhood and this was the release of the album," Ed Motta remembers, though he would have been only four years old. "The gig was pretty much like an A.A.C.M. [Chicago-based Association for the Advancement of Creative Musicians] gig, pretty much related to students and people from the religion. It wasn't a commercial gig. It was a very different environment."[2]

Playing to the converted is one thing, but if Rational Culture was really going to take off outside Rio de Janeiro, Tim was the guy to drum-up converts by taking the Tim Maia Racional show on the road. "The band was hot and ready to go!" Don Pi said. The band had the music covered, but the band's management had priorities other than managing the band and tour. "The Rational Culture managers seemed more interested in money and the beautiful girls who hung around Tim and the band than organizing a real tour," Pi recalls. In 1975, information didn't travel as fast as it does today, meaning many of Tim's fans had no clue about his conversion to Rational Culture, especially those outside of Rio de Janeiro who hadn't seen (or heard of) Tim personally evangelizing around town. For Rational Culture, this was a great opportunity to sell some books and records and maybe convert some irrational heathens.

The tour and Tim's involvement in Rational Culture ended unexpectedly and quickly following a disastrous show in the small town of Passa Quatro in Minas Gerais, about three hours from Rio. "As usual what concerned the cult was that before we do anything we must go to the temple and pray for hours," Pi

Figure 18 *Left to right: Elza Maria, Agenor Mendes Filho, Robson Jorge (obscured), Don Pi, Geraldo, Valdecir Nei Machado, Paulinho Guitarra, unknown roadie, and Tim Maia. Photo courtesy of Don Pi.*

remembers. "That was a big pain in the ass for me, and some of the other musicians, as well because I was already smoking grass [again] and having a good time. If Tim realized that one of us was high you would get fired right way without parole." Pi continues:

That day after the prayer ceremony, we jumped on the tour bus. When we arrived at this little city, the town was really full. People were expecting the great Tim Maia and band show, everybody did. And then the whole bullshit started: the sound system was a mess, the weather was shit, it was raining a lot. But for a little town like that, to have Tim Maia and band was just a big deal, an unforgettable occasion, so nobody cared about the rain.

When we began to do our sound check, I could see some guys around the stage talking shit about our [white] uniforms, looking at us like we were out of our minds. I commented to the bass player about that, and he also had the same impression. In between this time, Tim and the Rational Culture crew were going around town trying to gain more converts into the cult religion. They were going around and giving people flyers with the cult information and so on. By the time they came back, the place had about five or six thousand people waiting for the greatest concert of their lives.

Tim arrived backstage and ordered everybody to get ready, so we did, but when we started to play the first tune, most of audience had been already waiting a long time and wanted to hear the usual Tim Maia repertoire and that wasn't going to happen. After the second song, we got our first beer can thrown at us; people were angry and disappointed. We carried on until a large Black guy came in front of the stage with a huge rock in his hand screaming like crazy, demanding his favorite song. But Tim just didn't care about that guy and continued to sing the Rational songs. Then things got really ugly: the motherfucker jumped up on stage and encouraged the whole audience to join him as well. So, we had to pick up our instruments and get off the stage immediately, otherwise we would get killed—right then and there, live on stage, ho boy!

8 The Disenchantment

"Mystical phase, right [laughs]?" Tim responds to Ruy Castro's prompt about how he got into the Rational Culture from his 1991 *Playboy* interview with the singer. "I took fifty mescaline pills and wanted to be a member of the order of St. Francis of Assisi [laughs], peace and love, that hippie business: everyone would walk to Bahia . . . ."[1] Tim's response is clearly dismissive of his own agency and belief in Rational Culture, though as the interview continues, Tim connects his Rational Culture adventure to his lifelong interest in UFOs. "Rational Culture said it was a preparation for us to contact the extraterrestrials. As I'm into UFO stuff, I've been into it since I was a boy, and I got into this thing to see if it's really *it*, but it wasn't. It was business based on spiritualism, you know?"[2]

"When I got there [to Belford Roxo], I saw that the business was *Umbanda*, *Candomblé*, low spiritualism," Tim Maia recounts. Tibério blames Seu Manoel's family for Rational Culture's demise. Like all cults, movements, or new religions, once they gain enough success, money, or followers they will attract to it those who don't have the purest motives and over time their influence can corrupt the positivity that attracted followers initially. Tibério claims that this dynamic occurred with Seu Manoel and Rational Culture right around the time when Tim Maia joined. According to Tibério, seeing how popular *Universe in Disenchantment* had become, especially with the recruitment of Tim Maia, Seu Manoel's family members convinced him to serialize his single book into more and more volumes, eventually numbering one thousand. "The first one [original one] said it all," Tibério insists. "The other ones were repeating what was in the first one, divided into volumes in order to make money. When you do that, it loses its power. This was the influence of the family, the brother-in-law, everybody sucking Manoel Jacintho Coelho's money."

When Tim realized that Seu Manoel was not the deity he believed him to be, he slashed his ties with the leader and Rational Culture, and rarely talked about it for the remainder of his life. As hard as it is to understand why Tim, the ultimate skeptic, could go for this kind of thing, the reasons for his departure are a bit anti-climactic, depending on whose version you believe. Raphael, the Rational Culture website master and my Rational Culture contact, made a point of clarifying the following via a WhatsApp text following our first phone interview:

> Tim Maia stopped reading the book because of his financial interests that were not satisfied. He wanted a share in the sale of the books because he thought he was advertising the book through his records and the author said he [Seu Manoel] should read the book again, because the book is not for gaining profit. Tim Maia got angry and then stopping reading the book. That is the real reason that he never shared.[3]

Paulinho Guitarra calls it bullshit. "No, because it was an esoteric thing, something out of this world. It was a spacy thing, saying that we're from another planet. Finally, someone explained [to him] the origin of humanity, where we came from and what our destiny will be, but it was a mountain of lies!" Tim was spending lots of money and none of it was coming back to him, but even so, this fact only seemed to bother Tim after he changed his mind about Rational Culture. Tim's Rational albums, live concerts, press clippings, and public appearances all resulted in cash for Rational Culture or translated into book sales, as Tim recounted to Ruy Castro in *Playboy* in 1991: "I did about ten [Rational concerts]—paying for everything, buses and more buses. We'd go on television with the book in hand, and just like that, Jacintho sold 10,000 books. . . . The whole thing was about selling the book. That is why today I have this aversion to books, I do not read anything, not even comics."[4]

Responding to Rational Culture's "official" account of why Tim Maia parted ways with Seu Manoel, it seems unlikely he would ask for a cut of the book sales given his generosity toward the man and his community in Belford Roxo. Even if he did, once rejected, it seems unlikely it would have led Tim to quit Rational Culture. The most plausible explanation for his departure from Rational Culture has to do with something that changed Tim's thinking about Seu Manoel, the man, and it had nothing to do with money. "On the day that Tim became disillusioned with him, it was because he caught the old man messing with a girl," Tibério remembers referring to Seu Manoel.

"He was fucking everyone there," Tim said in the *Playboy* interview, "he was a sexual pervert and it was a totally sleazy scene," which says a lot coming from Tim.[5] "The people he screwed, started telling me: the owner of a horse farm, half of

Jacarepaguá [a neighborhood in Rio de Janeiro] and several contractors who made the Rio de Janeiro-Niterói Bridge," Tim says humorously exaggerating in classic Tim Maia style. Tim's loss of faith quickly shifted his attention to his loss of money, the money he donated to Rational Culture, some of which supposedly was channeled to "a huge property in Nova Iguaçu, which even included a motel for extraterrestrials."[6] The motel was for the Rational ancestors coming to pick us up from Earth, but seeing as it's such a long trip across the universe, naturally, they built a place for them to stay the night before taking the few, the proud, the demagnetized back home to a reunion with the Rational Superior.

"I told him, 'he's a man, Tim, he's not a eunuch, dammit,'" Tibério says. "With Tim it was too much, all the time." Tim was so obsessed with the books and reaching rational immunization that he didn't notice his guru was a dirty old man. "We knew that Manoel Jacintho Coelho was giving the wives and girlfriends of some guys some dirty looks," Paulinho says.

> Tim was surprised and confused to hear that Seu Manoel was fucking around. "I don't believe shit from that guy anymore." He was disillusioned and felt deceived. Manoel was not the guy Tim thought he was. When this happened, the band had already left [Rational Culture]. No one else lasted as long [as Tim], that many months, straight, living like that.

Don Pi, the young skeptic, claims he knew it all along. "The funny thing was that whenever I would try to talk about those issues [with Tim], somebody would call [Tim's apartment] from the Church in the name of the leader, Mr. Manoel and like a miracle,

Tim would change his mind immediately, it was just like he was brainwashed." It was a big change for a couple of wild and crazy musicians living the life in Rio de Janeiro; even "talking about sex was a big taboo because Mr. Manoel would tell us that sex is only valid if we do it with our wives or partners, but, he himself had several love affairs right at the temple!" Pi says he knew something wasn't right from his first visit there:

> It's not what Tim thinks it is. I could tell. There was something there, which doesn't match, not because the place was very poor or simple, there was some kind of aura there, a kinda atmosphere there, the way people moved there, the way people kinda looked up to money and stuff like that. It was a little suspicious. I didn't like it. But, hey, I was getting paid, I was with my idol and the music was just great. To be beside him was just like, "oh my god! I'm in paradise here, as a musician."

According to Nelson Motta, "Tim might be a little crazy, but he was not stupid." Despite the books he read, all the life changes and other concessions he'd made for Rational Culture, he still wasn't levitating or seeing aliens. "He was living in Belford Roxo, working like a madman, selling records on the street and singing for free on television, doing very few shows and those were mostly for Rational Culture followers, not smoking, not drinking, not fucking and not seeing the color of money," Nelson Motta writes. "His immunization must not be working; he had read seven books, but his life only got worse and he was definitively disenchanted with the universe of his Manoel Jacintho."[7] In one of the rare instances when Tim discussed this phase later in life, he told Tárik de Souza in *Jornal do Brasil* in 1982: "I ended up as a slave to that, recorded two preaching discs that made Manoel sell 40,000 Racional books. I appeared on Flávio Cavalcanti [popular TV program] all in white, regenerated, lean, a believer, almost destroyed as an artist."[8]

There's one other explanation that surfaced in my research that could help to explain Tim's sudden disillusionment and departure from Rational Culture. I attempted to confirm this story, inconclusively, and as you will read, Paulinho and Pi don't exactly agree on what actually happened. Don Pi explains that shortly before leaving Rational Culture, something strange, suspicious, and sad happened:

One day when we were there [at Belford Roxo] for some ceremony and Artulio, the oldest son of Seu Manoel, came drunk and under the influence of drugs—you could tell right away—he was upset and started screaming in the courtyard there, screaming that his father was a motherfucker and, "you guys will all find out what happened here, that there's thousands of dollars sitting there in the basement!"

Manoel Jacintho Coelho bought a huge brand new American car called a Galaxy and asked Artulio to drive somewhere to deliver these books. Then we heard that the guy had a car accident somewhere in the mountains between Minas Gerais and Rio. How come a brand-new car breaks like this? It came out that somebody set him up. Somebody set the boy up. He died. The car went up the hill and by the time he went down the brakes didn't work anymore. Nobody talks about this. A lot of people know this, but nobody will admit that this was really a betrayal and a set-up, but that's what happened. His father was all over it. It was a hit! And nobody knew if he was drunk or high [when the accident happened].

About a week later we went to play what would be the last Tim Maia Racional concert [in Passa Quatro, discussed in Chapter 7]. On the way there Tim was talking and was very upset about Artulio's death and nobody could answer his questions about where [they had buried] the body? And then we tried to play the concert. Normally, after every concert we'd go back there [Belford Roxo] and have some food and then pray again and then pay respect to Seu Manoel again and bring him the money, but this time, that never happened. We drove to Tim's house [in Copacabana] and that was exactly the moment when Tim started to open his eyes and said, "I'm not playing with this thing anymore!" And the guys went home, and I was there, and he was talking to me, even crying—I rarely saw him cry—and that night he was crying bitter tears, I mean he was really upset. "Something is wrong here, I mean, we'll go back there tomorrow and see this in the daylight, I gotta talk to these people again."

Paulinho Guitarra is not so sure there was any crime committed, and Artulio had been acting erratically, including public intoxication and belligerence, so a substance-induced accident is not entirely out of the question. "It was an accident," Paulinho says. "Manoel adored him, Tim adored him, everyone loved Artulio. I want to believe that it was an accident. Many people think many things. . . . There was no homicide. We were there, Tim, me, we were friends with the family. It was an accident; he was coming back to Rio and he crashed."

The next day, Tim went back to Belford Roxo to attempt to make sense of these rumors and Artulio's mysterious death. Don Pi was along for the trip as Tim's driver and he recounts

Figure 19 *Left to right: Artulio (son of Rational Culture founder), Tim Maia, Paulinho Guitarra, and João Roberto Kelly. Photo courtesy of Paulinho Guitarra.*

the scene from Tim's final visit to Belford Roxo and final meeting with Seu Manoel:

> When we got there, curiously, the place was almost empty, there were a few people there, it was ten, eleven o'clock in the morning, summer time, and then he disappeared inside the place there. He wasn't in there very long and then I saw him come out. I knew Tim, so when I saw him walking really fast, I knew something was wrong. He was a big guy and never walked fast. He said, "let's go, let's get the guitars and whatever you can grab in your hands and let's get out of here!" I said, "what happened?" He said, "I'll tell you later, let's get out of here!"

Tim and Pi are speeding away from Belford Roxo, Pi behind the wheel, Tim fuming and cursing, somewhere between furious and embarrassed. Guitars, cables, whatever they could grab running out of the Rational Culture compound on that sunny September morning were stuffed into the back seat and trunk of the Chevette on their ninety-minute drive back to Tim's apartment in Copacabana. That's a long time to think about what happened, where he went wrong, was it true these rumors about Artulio? Or was Tim more upset with Seu Manoel for his own magnetic and animalistic behavior, doing the same thing that so many religious leaders in positions of great power have done since the beginning of time, abusing their position for sexual satisfaction? Tibério, again, saw Tim's fault in his fanaticism; that he didn't realize that Seu Manoel was just a man, however special and mystical, but in the end, a mortal man:

> The great mistake Tim made with Seu Manoel was because he canonized him, he made him into a god, a saint. When he discovered he was actually a man and liked women, he was so pissed off with Seu Manoel. And then there was all of the money that Tim had donated and how it was being used, buying property and racing horses. Tim was left poor because [Seu Manoel] was taking all of the money he was paid, buying property in Barra and more for his mountain of children and grandchildren. So, on top of all of this falling on his shoulders, he sees the old man [with someone else's wife].

Just a year after tearing up his double record deal with RCA, the first Brazilian soul music artist given that opportunity, Tim Maia found himself nearly destitute, down to the trio of himself,

Don Pi, and Paulinho Guitarra, without a record contract or a gig on the horizon. As Pi recalls,

> We were broke, because Tim just donated a fortune to Rational Culture. He gave everything up. Our apartment [in Copacabana] was empty. When we came back from this mess we didn't have anything, even a pan to cook on in our apartment, because he donated everything to the religion. Everything. Acoustic guitar, equipment and P.A. system, everything was gone. And financially, we were broke.

Ed Motta remembers that even though the family might have not understood Uncle Tim's ways, "the family used to make a bit of a joke about it, but it was kinda serious because he was absolutely broke because he gave money to the religion, so it was super serious for him, that I know, and he was in a difficult situation after this." Don Pi picks up the story as Tim's white Chevette arrives back in Copacabana:

> We went back to Copacabana and from there he called Paulinho Guitarra and Beto Cajueiro and his wife [Ana Cristina Lins Cajueiro], as some people were still at their apartment selling books and making calls to sell books; their house was quite full. [After everyone arrived at Tim's Copacabana apartment], he was really upset and informed the group that he told Manoel Jacintho Coelho very clearly that he was out of this bullshit and, "if you guys want to stay, it's your problem." But nobody believed him and then he started talking about Artulio's death, but nobody believed because people were really possessed by this thing, as he also was before this happened. And the following

day he made the final decision not to go back again. It shocked everybody, but it didn't shock me. And that was the time he said to me, and the people there, "you can do me a favor, before you go home, pack up all these [Rational Culture] things and put them in your cars and get these things out of my apartment." His apartment was full [of books and records].

Consider Tim's band's perspective: even if you were faking the funk like Pi was, nobody knew if Tim was going to change his mind back the very next day. "The day after, he said, 'you know what? Let's go to the *churrascaria* [Brazilian BBQ],'" Pi remembers. "'I'm feeling like eating some heavy food and smoking a joint and I wanna go buy myself a bottle of whiskey,' and from that time I knew it was clear, he had really quit."

Cutting back to the opening scene of this book where Tim is yelling from his balcony, Nelson Motta captured a different part of the incendiary monologue, particularly this graphic indictment of Seu Manoel, delivered loudly and under the influence by a half-naked Tim from his open window overlooking Copacabana:

This Manoel Jacintho does not deceive me, he spent 15 years training with the witch *Seu Sete da Lira* [a manifestation of Exu, an Afro-Brazilian deity] and owns a huge property in Nova Iguaçu, which even has a motel for extraterrestrials. He takes *guiné-tatu*, a root that leaves the person wanting sex for three days without stopping, it could be that his flag waves until he's 90. He's the king of *guiné-tatu* and fucked all the little girls, putting a sheep in each house [a unique Tim Maia-ism with an unknown meaning, but it probably means something like, "with a bun in every oven"]. And he's saying that women magnetize!

What Nelson failed to document, probably because he wasn't there, was what Don Pi described happening right after Tim completed his drunken balcony diatribe:

> I remember it as yesterday, it was a summer day, sunshine, 38 degrees [Celsius = 100 degrees Fahrenheit], blue sky and in a minute, it was cloudy and then it started to explode everywhere, in a space of ten minutes, it started to rain heavily, and everybody was like, "oh my god, this is the punishment!" And I was like, "no man, we didn't see before that there was a cloud coming [from behind us] already. . . . This is the way it is in summertime; yesterday was like that too," but everyone was devastated and scared and quiet and I was laughing!

For some band members, the drama was the price to play with their idol, Tim Maia. "The music was just so great. We had a great time there even with this religious cult, but nobody cared," Pi says.

> I didn't care [about Rational Culture] when we were rehearsing there [at the shed] with a huge view of Ipanema, the lagoon, Leblon and Jesus Christ [the Cristo Redentor statue] there. The rehearsal space was all open and he had like 32 dogs there and the dogs were running free in the back and the front yard, and all the windows and doors open and this beautiful, huge view.

Don Pi was the last man standing when Tim finished with his Rational experiment. Even though he didn't believe in these things, he was Tim's roommate, errand boy, in-house soundman, maid, and joint-roller. As Pi tells it:

After the rehearsal, everyone would go home because most of the band lived in Niterói at that time and I was the one who stayed, and we would go back to Copacabana. I was living with the guy. I was waking up with him and with him until he goes to his room [at night], I go to my room and in the middle of the night if Tim wakes up and feels like smoking something he'd wake me up and then we started playing music, or eating, having fun, we might call some girls, stuff like this.

Life quickly returned to pre-Rational conditions back at Tim's Copacabana apartment. Within days of their exodus from Belford Roxo, Pi remembers:

I went to Mangueira, up on the hill there in the favela, to get some grass [marijuana]. I couldn't find the good one he likes, but it didn't matter, he was taking any kind after that long— and I brought some bullshit back and he was like, "it doesn't matter, let's have a party!" And I go to Gordon's and buy some hamburgers and cheeseburgers. . . . That guy was a radical with whatever he did. He was very straight in Rational Culture, but Tim never had a middle point, where you could say "now he's balanced." He was either way up here or way down there. When he went for something, he went for it heavy! He didn't have a take it easy approach. He was a party-man. And a few days later we started to clean the apartment.

No thorough investigation of Tim's Rational recordings should fail to discuss the handful of Rational Culture singles released by Tim's label, Seroma, during this short period of time. There are a handful of Rational Culture singles, released on seven-inch records, but unlike singles in the United States, in Brazil they play, like LPs, at 33 rpms and also like their twelve-inch siblings have small spindle holes. There are at least three Rational Culture–related singles released on Seroma, with varying levels of involvement from Tim. There's the four-song EP with edited versions of songs from the first LP, there's nothing new or unreleased here, just edited versions of "Rational Culture" and "Bom Senso."

Tim Maia Racional e Coro Racional (Seroma-0001) is an odd release and doesn't seem like Tim had much to do this one at all, with its old-timey marching music and trumpeting horns, except for one song, "O Grão Mestre Varonil," a title that also appears on *Tim Maia Racional* Vol. 1. In Tim's LP version, the song is a twenty-second a cappella tribute to Manoel Jacintho Coelho. The song that appears on this single is nearly three minutes long, starting with the same exact vocals from Tim's LP version, which appear to be then spliced with a choir (Portuguese *coro*), who Paulinho Guitarra remembers being called Racionais Do Samba, singing Tim's lyrics without his involvement. That's the extent of Tim's participation for that one. The cover is also simpler than the previous single with a stark white design with the yellow portal image and the same followers looking up to the unusually tall person.

The only other known Seroma Rational release is credited to Grupo Vangarda Show (Seroma CSR-001) and contains no explicit reference to Tim Maia at all other than its provenance on his Seroma label looking just like a miniature version of one of his LP jackets. The song on the A-side "Desencanto Universal" (Universal Disenchantment) sounds closer to Tim's music with its spacy synthesizers and groovy down-tempo rhythm track. Side

B is titled "Hino Racional" (Rational Anthem) and exudes as much excitement as you might expect from an existential hymn. Those are all the Tim Maia Rational related singles on Seroma until Don Pi told me about some of these boxes of records he took back to his mom's house at the end of Tim's Rational Culture detour.

One morning very soon after Tim's return to his normal, irrational state, Pi was about to leave town for a week after all of this craziness—remember he's only nineteen years old at the time—to visit his family. Tim bought Pi a *Fuscinha*, what they call a Volkswagen Beetle in Brazil, and asked him for one last favor:

> "You know what, go on down to the cellar and there's a lot of boxes, throw them all away. I don't want to see them ever again!" And I did it. I didn't know that years later this [record] was going to be something that people wanted to have. But I kept two boxes of LPs and three boxes of *compactos* [seven-inch singles], which are quite rare, and nobody has. This is a very special thing. We recorded it before we jumped out of the thing. . . . What happened is we recorded this *compacto* without knowing what was going to happen and three months later and it was ready with a cover and everything. . . . I put [the boxes] in the *fuscinha* and took them to my mother's house.

While this still cannot be confirmed, because these boxes are still in storage at Pi's family's home in Barra Mansa, what he describes is another Seroma single, recorded during Tim's Rational phase, pressed and sleeved in similar Rational Culture emblazoned sleeves, but never officially distributed or released, because the final product arrived at Tim's house within days of Tim's departure from Rational Culture.[9]

9 Irrational and Loving It

The new conditioning of someone who has joined a religious movement has overcome the previous 20 or 30 years of parental and other societal conditioning. Once it is in place, it can be very difficult to shake. The member not only has the new set of beliefs, which he has learnt in such a way that they are internally consistent and completely logical; he has also become bonded to a new set of friends; he has also had a powerful religious experience; he has learnt to revere and love the prophet or founder of the religion and his (or more rarely her) teachings; he has also forged a strong new commitment to God. All of this is very real. To expect him simply to be able to throw it all away and return to the "normal" religion of his youth, without a titanic inner struggle, is unrealistic.

DAVID V. BARRETT, *THE NEW BELIEVERS*[1]

Consider these final three chapters as important postscripts to the story of *Tim Maia Racional and Tim Maia Racional* Vol. 2. The first addresses Tim's recordings immediately following his departure from Rational Culture, all of which belong to Tim's Seroma era and contain clues, lyrics, notes, and allusions to help us understand what Tim thought about his time with Rational Culture. Seeing as he rarely ever spoke about these seventeen months, the tidbits of information excavated from these albums are as close as we can now get to Tim's perspective on his existential adventure. Tim was prolific in the months following his exit, despite being broke, recording one single and three albums between leaving Rational Culture in September 1975 and the end of 1976. The penultimate chapter explores the rediscovery of these albums in the 1990s by Marisa Monte, Gal Costa, Racionais MCs, Marcelo D2, and a record dealer named Rodrigo Piza. The final chapter explores the complicated and fascinating discovery and recreation of what might have been Tim Maia's third Rational album, what eventually was released in 2012 as *Tim Maia Racional* Vol. 3 and the lingering complications surrounding Tim Maia's estate.

In late 1975 Tim was broke, but free from Rational Culture. Anger and a determination to recover what he'd lost fueled Tim's intense drive over the coming months. A renewed love affair with booze, drugs, and women helped stimulate his overflowing creativity. "His disillusionment was proportional to his fanaticism," Tibério says, noting that when he returned to his pre-Rational, hedonistic lifestyle, he did so with extra gusto, trying to make up for over a year of lost time not having fun. "He was so fanatical, so he changed instead to dive into chaos." Tim exorcized his demons musically in the most soulful way across one single and three albums he and the Seroma Band recorded in the last months of 1975 and early 1976, the single "Ela Partiu," *Tim Maia* a.k.a. "The English Album" (Seroma 1975/8),[2] *Tim Maia* (Som Livre, 1976/7), and *Tim Maia* (Polydor, 1976).

In late 1975 and early 1976, money, or the lack of it, was a serious problem for Tim with almost all of his reserves depleted, not to mention nearly all of his worldly possessions. And then they lost the Copacabana apartment on Figueiredo de Magalhães street, moving temporarily to the *Barracão*, which would only do for a while as it didn't have a kitchen or the basics for extended habitation. "The situation was ugly, Tim began to pawn his instruments: guitars, bass, saxophone, and the flute he bought in the United States, it all got pawned. With the first money that came in he went back and rescued [the instruments]," Nelson Motta writes.[3] Looking to make some quick cash Tim lined up some shows, however small given his tarnished reputation, with the remaining band members: Paulinho on guitar, Pi on keyboards, a friend of Paulinho's from Niterói, Carlos Simões, on bass, and on drums, the much respected Paulinho Braga, who Tim had known for years. During this formation's rehearsals, Tim led the band from behind the drum kit.

The first of Tim's releases with Tim playing drums was his very next single, the first release after Tim's departure from Rational Culture, "Ela Partiu" backed with "Meus Inimigos." Given its vintage and stark, moody groove, it sounds like an existential crisis dressed up like a break-up song, where Tim sings as if his loss is far darker and profound than romantic love. "Everybody thinks that," Pi says, contradicting my theory.

> It's about the mother of his son, it's about Carmelo Maia's mother, Geisa. At that time Carmelo was already one year old. . . . When Geisa left, that song was composed for her, because she left him, though she did come back like two years later. And in between she used to come back and go to see Carmelo and they'd get together and sleep together.

According to Pi, the song was actually composed during Tim's Rational phase, the time Geisa left him while he and Don Pi were still with Rational Culture but wasn't recorded until right after he quit in late 1975 at Rio de Janeiro's Transamérica Studios. Given its later vintage, after leaving Rational Culture, perhaps there's hope for my theory yet, that Tim channeled his existential angst, frustration, and betrayal through this tough-as-nails soul ballad, so powerful in its desperation. It's a heart-on-your-sleeve song of defeat, but instead of leaving the listener depressed and weary, Tim, like the mythical Phoenix, is reborn in his own defeat. Tim thrived in chaos, however painful it was for him and those around him at the time. "It was a big shock for him and a lot of trouble for me," Pi writes:

> I say trouble because as his roommate and best friend at the time I had to listen to his crying, smoking lots of weed, drinking and so on. At that same time, it was amazing to see how creative he became because that was exactly when he would take his guitar and with me on keyboards would sing any kind of melody, playing any choruses that came to him with his eyes closed and finally jumping up to say: "mother fucker, I got it!" I thought he was mad at me but no, he was just getting a new song together. "Ela Partiu" was one of many songs he composed for her, talking about her going away and never coming back. A few weeks later we were in the studio to record this![4]

"Meus Inimigos" (My Enemies) shows Tim getting back to that "Réu Confesso" and "Gostava Tanto De Você" samba-soul groove with lyrics delivered so warmly, if you didn't speak Portuguese you probably wouldn't guess the drama hinted at in the song's title. Singing sweetly and soulfully, Tim warns the listener that his enemies will tell stories to sabotage him, but just come with him and hear his version of the story. This song proves that he could return musically to his 1973 samba-soul style without breaking a sweat. This single, the only non-Rational Seroma single released during the Seroma years, has a special co-star that needs to be called out: Tim's drumming. Between the sophisticated and swinging samba-soul groove laid down on "Meus Inimigos" to the restrained yet powerful drumming on "Ela Partiu" (I especially love his machine-gun like drum fill at 3:34), Tim reminds us that he started his musical journey behind the drum kit. The original Seroma single is one of Tim's rarest releases, probably due to its extremely limited pressing paid for with whatever money Tim managed to scrounge up at that time.

Despite living on the verge of poverty in Rio de Janeiro, Tim's plan for financial and reputational recovery had him focused on the birthplace of soul music. Deep in the hole financially, Tim decided to go for the long odds with what little money he had left. Tim was going to record an album entirely in English! Tim's bet was that some gringo in New York, Los Angeles, or London would hear his English-language debut and decide to break him in the homeland of soul music, placing him to toe-to-toe with his idols and the only musicians he deemed to be his real competition. Pi confirms this theory: "Exactly, that's exactly what he thought, because of the time he spent there. He was a teenager when he went to the U.S. and years later he came up with this idea to record a whole album in English."

Having reached the highest levels within three years of his first album, Tim sought a greater challenge, a more difficult target. "International music, I think is much better, much more playable, more conscious, more musical. American music has become international music, everyone understands this music . . . . I think that's the music that I play," Tim says, sounding like his nephew, Ed Motta, who's come under considerable scrutiny in recent years for saying similarly sensitive things about Brazil's place in global pop culture and its insular nature. "Brazilian music, I sometimes play it, but I don't play it a lot, I play it because I can," Tim said in the same interview.[5]

The music on this English-language album, titled *Tim Maia,* is fantastic and an underappreciated jewel in Tim's catalog. Possibly emboldened by the more biographical lyrics from the Rational albums, namely "Bom Senso," Tim experimented with new lyrical topics on "Let's Have a Ball Tonight". Except for his Rational recordings, this is his first overtly political song and the first to draw on his own life (outside of his love life and favorite foods). Certain that his English album would kick-start his international career, a message song like this one was perfectly aligned with the radical American soul and funk zeitgeist and was right in step with his idols the Isely Brothers, who released *The Heat Is On* with its incendiary funk jam "Fight the Power," and Curtis Mayfield who released (*There's No Place Like) America Today*, both in 1975. Beyond the noteworthiness of the content, what's striking about this song's lyrics is the emotional, spiritual, and existential catharsis on display over a grown and sexy funk groove. Collectively, these albums show Tim processing his disappointment, confusion, and lust for life as he wrestled with his own existential embarrassment for having sunk so deeply into Seu Manoel's bizarre world.

By early 1976, Tim had never sunk so low professionally. It must have been a harsh reminder of his pre-fame struggles not so many years ago in São Paulo. "We were broke, we didn't have money even for food, gasoline, or anything. Despite his name and fame no record labels wanted to have anything to do with Tim Maia," Don Pi remembers.[6] The desperation and darkness comes through in the Seroma band's funk vamps, tighter than ever in their lean line-up. "The Rational phase, it was a big loss," Paulinho Guitarra says. "Tim Maia didn't earn any money, the band didn't earn any money, people didn't book us for shows, it was a loss. The money was gone."

Both Pi and Paulinho agree that the album was a horrible financial decision, but both also consider it a personal favorite, because of its intimate setting, stripped of the excesses of the pre-Rational days and the fanaticism of the Rational albums. It was just four dudes rehearsing their asses off to prepare the album that they hoped would save Tim's career. Later they descended on Somil studios (the same studio where *Rational* Vol. 1 and 2 were completed and where *Rational* Vol. 3 was recorded) recording the songs live in the studio to save on costs. Paulinho reflects on the making of this album:

> That left me and Pi; Pi and me. I had a bassist, Carlos Simões, who lived in Niterói and was a great bassist. We had a rock band together. I said, "come on and let's play with Tim." We rehearsed and then went to the studio and recorded [the album] live. It was our *Kind of Blue*. Tim recorded his vocals later, but a lot of things happened in the moment.

"On the other hand, the band, now reduced to about four musicians . . . we used to play all day long non-stop, taking a break only for lunch or to smoke a joint. It was a lot of fun!"

Looking at the back-cover photo, Pi points something out: "The only person there [on the back cover] with a blue t-shirt is me, everybody else is still dressed in white, because everybody was too scared to take their white shirts off!"[7]

"I took this photo [of Tim Maia behind the drum kit] and he took a photo of me in the same place in the Seroma studios," Paulinho remembers. "Originally, Tim wanted to make a gatefold cover for the English album full of photos of the band, but lots of them [photos] came out kinda bad. The photos are not professional, because we didn't have any money. Tim was the drummer [on this album] and sang, so that's why he's behind the drums in this photo. 'I'm a drummer, man!'" This album and the contemporaneous single "Ela Partiu" are the

Figure 20 *Tim Maia behind the drum kit for what was supposed to be included in the gatefold cover for Tim's 1976 English language album. Photo courtesy of Paulinho Guitarra.*

first professional recordings where Tim played drums and they wouldn't be his last.

"I made an English LP for export," Tim told Tárik de Souza in 1982. "I could not send the record there, nor distribute it here. I was totally beached."[8] Running on financial fumes, they finished recording the album and sent the now-simplified covers to the printer. Without enough money to pay for the record pressing, Tim and band resorted to selling the covers alone as down payment on the future record, which the buyer could collect after it was pressed! And to make matters worse, without the help of the Rational Culture crew, their sales team was reduced to just the four band members selling the album door-to-door.

The LP jackets sat stacked in boxes in Tim's closets for a year or more, until Tim could afford to press the LPs and properly release the album, but by 1978 (the year most discographies attribute to this album's release though no date appears on the record label or sleeve) Tim had already released a couple more albums and the raw, minimal sound of these sessions were now completely out of sync with the late 1970s' disco spirit.

With his career-rescuing English-language album stillborn on arrival, Tim appeared to resort to some classic hustler tricks. Bursting with new music rehearsed and ready to go, Tim contacted Gazeta Studios in São Paulo to track some more new songs. Why São Paulo? Maybe the band was gigging there or likely all the studios around Rio knew Tim was broke, but maybe word hadn't reached São Paulo yet. Either way, Tim and the same Seroma band from the English album with the addition of Paulo Roquete on second guitar and background vocals recorded a majority of the backing tracks for another new Tim Maia album in São Paulo in early 1976. With the tight schedule to keep at the recording studio, Tim didn't have time to record his vocals or write, arrange, and record the horns and string parts. To Gazeta Studios' surprise and disappointment, Tim's sessions were not being bankrolled by a record label, so when he left for Rio without money to pay for the tapes, he had to leave them there.

Clearly, productivity was not Tim's problem at this critical juncture, it was money. He needed money to press up the vinyl for his English-language album, he needed money to release his São Paulo tapes from carbonite and a little more to finish that album with the requisite vocals, horns, and strings. "That's when from out of the sky a contract fell on Tim from Pedrinho da Luz," Nelson Motta writes, "who had replaced Jairo Pires as the artistic director for Polygram, the new name of the old Polydor, and with this offer, Tim could rest for a few months and pay to get the English record on Seroma pressed." With the offer from Polygram, Tim found some financial footing and a symbolic renaissance, signing to the same label he dumped right before getting into Rational Culture. Tim's 1976 album for Polygram is a fitting bookend to his Rational Culture years and a wonderful end to his legendary Seroma band. The funky philosophizing on "Nobody Can Live Forever" alludes to Tim's disappointment in not finding life's answers in Rational Culture, coldly denouncing God, the devil, and anything he can't touch, feel, see, or smell. This is not your average pop, soul, or even funk song, especially in Brazil, a country that is culturally very Catholic.

With Polygram's resources at his disposal, Tim got the full band back together with the full count coming to eleven musicians, including two bass players, two guitar players, keyboards, backing vocals, and a horn section. "We would meet at Seroma studios … and play all day long. It was fun because he used to provoke us by saying that the Black bass player was playing better than the white bass player, or the opposite. This made a kind of sweet fight between all the musicians and made the music groove like a big band, one trying to play better than the other." "Brother, Father, Sister, Mother," a song about humanity's tendency to seek solace in unhealthy ways and the need for more decency, emerged from one of these marathon rehearsals. Pi recalls:

> One day, after a long rehearsal period, Tim started to play a groove alone on drums, which sounded like disco music, and started to sing a kind of rap. He took a piece of paper and began writing the lyrics and forming the melody. He picked up the guitar and played the harmony and blew everyone's minds.

The album wasn't a runaway success, but it proved to those who heard it, that the King of Brazilian soul was back and sane, kind of. Though not released as a single, most Brazilians know this album as the one with "Rodésia" on it, the song's title being the name of the country now known as Zimbabwe with Tim's lyrics urging his African brothers to raise their heads and take what's theirs.

Out of rational hibernation and ready to jam and party (in equal parts), Tim announced his return to the social scene and reassumed his throne at Seroma headquarters, *O Barracão*, holding court for all of his band and any onlookers who cared to see if he was really "himself" again. His old friends, who'd grown tired of his Rational routine, were back, like Tibério Gaspar and Hyldon, as well as the usual Brazilian soul soldiers, like Fábio, who wrote in his book: "That beautiful place would be the scene of many meetings, projects and unforgettable rehearsals. Many friends visited him: Tibério Gaspar, Guillerme Lamounier, Lincoln Olivetti, Nonato Buzar, vocalists Solange, Lidiani, Lilian, Jussara, Cristina Conrado and Eliane Martins."

"Every day, these guys would show up to play, talk, learn and enjoy our music. Sometimes we'd have a full place, which looked like a live concert," Don Pi remembers.

> When that happened, Tim loved to really play a live concert; and of course, he loved to show everyone that he's the boss. If a musician played a wrong note or even played some strange choruses, he would stop the music right away and say, "hey my man, what the fuck are you doing, bro? Who do you think you are? I am the star here. Fuck that shit, play fewer notes boy, come on now!"

It's easy to imagine this different scene at the shed with Tim and a small band locked into a heavy funk groove while Tim's young sons Márcio Leonardo and Telmo play at his feet. The song "Márcio Leonardo & Telmo" is a simple funk riff built around a bouncing bass line and Pi's constant clavinet that gives a brief, yet joyous peek at Tim during this happy time in his life surrounded by family, friends, and his dogs. The photo from the back cover of this album captures Tim and his musical family behind the shed, posing on some rocks, Léo perched on his adopted father's knee holding a toy guitar.

The song "The Dance Is Over" was started by Don Pi and finished with musical assistance from Hyldon and English-language lyrical assistance from Tim, as Pi remembers:

I showed him a few choruses together with the melody, but he didn't like that I was playing a lot of harmonies; he hated lots of harmonies. So, I started to do something simpler, kind of a bossa nova groove. The other problem was that I only had the first part of the song; I was missing the rest. That's when Hyldon arrived from New York, back from a vacation. I showed him what I had done while Tim was taking a siesta in the corner [with a female friend] and making lots of noise [laughs]. Hyldon loved it right away and picked up the guitar and composed a second part of the song. Then we needed a kind of bridge to complete the song, cause only two parts was not going to make the man happy, right? At that time, we used to listen to the Isely Brothers a lot, loving the guitar player with those rock solos [Ernie Isely] and things like that. After Tim finished his nap, we showed him what we did and suggested some sort of Isely Brothers groove. He loved it and he immediately sat down at the drums and started to play this rock beat. You can listen to how he finishes the song by giving Paulinho Guitarra a full bridge to take his solo.

This tune is a fitting coda for Tim's legendary Seroma era and band, coming, naturally, as the last song on Tim's 1976 Polydor album, the final album recorded with the core Seroma team. With its topical lyrics, collaborative composition drawing on the tremendous skills of Don Pi, Paulinho Guitarra, and Seroma regular, Hyldon, it typifies Tim's sound from this time, straddling soul, funk, Latin and Brazilian styles, pushing Brazilian pop music well beyond its comfort zone and raising the bar for the Brazilian soul genre. It's Ed Motta's favorite song of his uncle's and given Ed's appreciation of jazz and sophisticated pop music, this endorsement is not lightweight: "The feel to it is very cool."[9] The song's English lyrics, in their haiku-like simplicity, sum up Tim's life lesson from his Rational phase:

> The Dance Is Over
> Face reality
> Forget the sorrows,
> There's a lot to live
> Have a ball
> While you can
> There's a lot to romance

Though recorded before the 1976 Polydor album, the album Tim started in São Paulo eventually saw its release on Som Livre in 1977, as, you guessed it, *Tim Maia*. The album is clearly a part with the English-language album, more than its 1977 release date suggests, featuring the same exact band with Tim behind the drum kit, plus Paulinho Roquete on guitar. There are also a few clues on the back cover that prove its earlier provenance. First, Tim's bolded note at the very end of the technical details: "The songs were composed, arranged, and rehearsed at the Seroma studios in front of the Rodrigues de Freitas Lagoon, one hundred meters above sea level. What a beauty!" This album is transitional in that it introduces a new name for Tim's band. "Seroma" was out as Tim announced a new name for his revolving cast of musicians, the Vitória Régia band, a name he would use for his bands for many years. The other clue was not subtle nor was it explicit, but it's the closest Tim came to sharing his feelings publicly about his previous two years. Appearing at the very top of the back cover of this release:

What I learned is that I learned that I didn't learn anything. Lots of things don't exist that they say exist. What exists is right here and we can't see.

For me the most important people are the children (because they represent the future). However, if misguided they will be lost, like us, in the middle of lies.

TIM MAIA[10]

Don Pi and Paulinho were getting tired of Tim's outbursts and out of control behavior. Paulinho Guitarra quit the band and severed his friendship with his boss and former idol just before Tim's 1978 album *Tim Maia Disco Club* (Atlantic, 1978). The band continued to be called Vitória Régia as they were on the last album released on Som Livre, but it wasn't the same without Paulinho there and others soon followed, including Don Pi a couple albums later. With the arrival of *Saturday Night Fever* in Brazil, just as in the United States, Brazilian soul and funk found its way on to the dancefloor, resulting in another fantastic tear of Tim Maia albums between 1978 and 1982, mostly produced by Lincoln Olivetti and former Seroma and Rational band veteran, Robson Jorge.

Like most black musicians, Tim saw disco music for what it was—syncopated funk music that white people could dance to—and he said as much in an interview following the success of his *Disco Club* album: "I make Black music. And Blacks need to be convinced that they're coming to the white world accidentally, in black galleons. Look, this movement they call 'Black Rio': these Blacks are not photocopies of the Americans.... You can't deny that this whole thing goes back to Africa."[11] Just a few years later, Tim had this to say about the producer who helped revive his career with *Tim Maia Disco Club*, claiming that Lincoln Olivetti's productions resembled those of Earth, Wind & Fire: "It's actually a copy of the copy because they're copying the Brazilian swing."[12]

Another self-released album from 1982, *Nuvens* (Clouds) (Seroma, 1982) is an overlooked classic. His last great album, *Descobridor dos Sete Mares* (Discoverer of the Seven Seas) (Lança, 1983), returned him to the top of the charts with an even mix of disco and quiet-stormers. Throughout Tim's career, his albums included a mix of up-tempo, party jams and sentimental torch songs, satisfying the young and the old, the ladies and the guys, or as Tim explained it: "Half of my songs are armpit-soakers and the other half are panty-soakers."[13] With the 1980s in full-swing, coke, paranoia, and re-recordings of his classic hits turned Tim into an occasionally profitable, yet unreliable, caricature of himself. Despite his notoriety for missing shows and sabotaging his own recording sessions, Tim continued to receive invitations to perform and record for the simple reason that when he was focused and sober enough, he could put on a masterful show or record a chart-topping hit. It just depended on what day you caught him and how badly he needed the money. Tim managed to achieve one of the greatest accolades for an aging star: he became a hero to the next generation. The rising pop star Cazuza referred to Tim as the "Punk of Funk," elaborating that "Tim Maia is one of the greatest Brazilian artists; he's the funniest, most disrespectful character and an authentic punk."[14]

The irony of Tim's post-Rational revelation is that he now felt liberated and even vindicated to go back to his instincts of a life built around satisfactions of the flesh, but this same revelation was also his death sentence, delivered bottle by bottle, cocaine line after cocaine line over the next dozen years, certainly leading to his premature death. Raphael from Rational Culture points out the obvious, the benefit that certainly did help Tim, because, "when he left, his health worsened, all of the drugs and twenty-three years later he died in 1998. When people die at fifty some years [it's clear that] they did not really care for their health."[15]

It wasn't until the mid-1990s that Tim Maia made his first ever visit to the doctor only to learn how much medical trouble he was in. Maybe he knew his time was running out, because in his last few years he revisited places and themes from earlier in his life. His final albums captured Tim interpreting bossa nova standards to much critical acclaim, and he spent more and more time at home with his menagerie of animals (dogs, goats and cows) and regularly hosting the kids from a nearby orphanage at his pool.

On March 15, 1998, Tim Maia's excessive lifestyle caught up with him after collapsing onstage a week earlier. He was fifty-five years old. His contribution to Brazilian music is only recently being fully appreciated as younger musicians and DJs begin to mine the better part of his thirty-year catalog. He redefined what it was to be a black Brazilian performer, singer, and bandleader. He was one of the first Brazilian musicians to own his own publishing company and record label, but most importantly, he pioneered a new genre of Brazilian music and created the ultimate "cult" records.

10 Rational Legacy

Rocking the backyard barbecue party, the place erupts,
When we drop the sound of Tim Maia Racional
MARCELO D2 FROM "O IMPÉRIO CONTRA-ATACA"[1]

Brazil's decades-long dictatorship came to an end in 1985, around the same time that the country's musical tastes shifted, like in the United States, away from the disco and R&B-dominated pop of the 1970s and early 1980s toward a rock and new-wave pop landscape. Tim Maia's classics still played on the radio and he scored a few more romantic hits in the final years of the 1980s, but the Black Rio movement he'd helped to start was all but gone, having fled for the favelas and transformed itself into indigenous hip-hop and *baile funk*. In 1991, Tim lamented the state of Brazilian music in the early 1990s:

> There's no band. There was Banda Black Rio, but now even Blacks together can't cut it. And the quality of the Brazilian musician is falling. He was considered one of the best musicians in the world, but the good ones have already left: Antonio Adolfo, Sergio Mendes, Eumir Deodato, Paulinho da Costa . . . have been in the United States for some time. A second team is left here, which is monopolized by the Recareys[2] of life agreeing to work for half the amount. Then they die of starvation. People often say, "Tim Maia complains," but someone has to complain. The

musicians are getting bad because they do not study enough, they do not have instruments and they don't practice. I'm having problems now with my new repertoire of bossa nova because those who play bossa nova do not play funk, and those who play funk do not play bossa nova—they do not have the skills to play samba, the samba swing comes from the guitar and its own kind of drums. Bossa nova is a sophisticated samba from the Zona Sul [Rio's famous beach neighborhoods of Copacabana, Ipanema, Leblon, and so on.], but it's samba, and this, the rockers do not really know. The quality of the musicians is falling because Brazilians are totally influenced by this tired rock that gets played everywhere. Even if you were influenced by Stevie Wonder or even Prince.[3]

Tim's pop culture presence during the 1980s and 1990s consisted of a handful of classic tunes revolving on Brazil's oldies radio, a few disco-era hits and some ill-advised yet surprisingly successful remakes of his earlier hits. A *paulista* friend of mine, David Galasse, born in the mid-1970s to lower-middle-class European immigrants, describes his early memories of Tim Maia's music:

Tim Maia was always present on the radio. It was impossible not to know at least five or six of his greatest hits. In the late eighties, all we heard from Tim Maia came from collections with really terrible artwork, mostly romantic songs like "Essa Tal Felicidade" (That Much Happiness) or "Me De Motivo" (Give Me Reason) and some sambas like "Aquele Abraço" [That Embrace] and "A Rã" [The Toad, the latter two being covers of songs by Gilberto Gil, João Donato and Caetano Veloso, respectively].

Some songs from his disco phase, such as "Acenda o Farol" (Turn on the Streetlight), "Sossego" (Peace & Quiet) and "A Fim de

Voltar" (In Order to Finish) played on the radio. At family parties, when everybody was drunk enough, my forty-something uncles loved to dance to "Descobridor dos Sete Mares" (The Discoverer of the Seven Seas) and [the 1980s remake of] "Não Quero Dinheiro" (I Don't Want Money).

Tim's refusal to talk about his Rational recordings and his caustic relationship with his past record labels resulted in his back catalog of classic music being limited if not completely out public circulation for much of the 1980s and 1990s, making some sense of his decision to rerecord his classic 1970s hits. But what about the Rational albums? Surely someone remembered them. Thanks to a couple female fans and friends of Tim's (Marisa Monte and Gal Costa) along with pioneering Brazilian hip-hop heroes Racionais MCs and Marcelo D2, as well as some entrepreneurial Tim Maia fans, the legend of Tim Maia Rational lived again, beginning in the 1990s, just before Tim's death.

In 1989, Marisa Monte's debut album, *MM*, dominated the Brazilian pop charts, heralding a return to a more nuanced and sophisticated pop sound equally indebted to Elis Regina, who she resembled in many ways, and to Tim Maia, who Monte considered a friend. One of the biggest hits from this album, produced by Nelson Motta, was Tim's tribute to one of his favorite foods: Chocolate. Marisa's version takes Tim's innocent ode to the deliciously sweet stimulant and inserts some other addictive indulgences, like snuff, cocaine, and her explicit call to "legalize marijuana," which certainly endeared her to Tim. Tim adored Marisa Monte, inviting her often to visit with him, referring to her as he did with many close friends, calling her by her full name, strung together tightly. Nelson Motta describes one of their interactions:

> On one of these visits, while knowing that Tim hated anything related to Rational Culture, Marisa wasn't afraid to tell him that she'd been singing "Que Beleza" during her shows and the audience was loving it. And she sang it for him. Tim wasn't mad, nor did he ask her to stop, he just grunted, "leave that alone, Marisamonte," and changed the subject.[4]

Presumably, the only reason she didn't record her own version of this song was due to the fact that in Brazil, one needs the original author's approval in order to record a cover version of their song. That's likely why, the very same year that Tim Maia died, his old friend and Tropicália veteran, Gal Costa, recorded a version of "Immunização Racional (Que Beleza)," the first popular cover of a song from Tim's Rational Culture period for her album *Aquele Frevo Axé*. When asked by the São Paulo newspaper, *A Folha De São Paulo*, if Tim would approve of her decision to record the song, she said, "I don't know. Probably [laughs], he loved to make a scandal. But I bet he's happy up there."[5]

For many young people growing up in Brazil's many metropolises, be it São Paulo, Rio de Janeiro, or any number of cities, Tim Maia's revival and especially the reverence for the Rational albums, were an underground phenomenon. "In the late nineties and early two-thousands, we used to go to nightclubs like Jive and Teatro Mars, to dance to samba-rock, funk, boogaloo and Brazilian music from the seventies," David Galasse reminisces. "That's the time I heard *Tim Maia Racional* for the first time and it was a total shock. I could not believe no one had shown me that before." Just as much as we can thank the DJs, hip-hop pioneers, and record collectors for Tim's Rational renaissance, it's the Davids and his friends and friends of friends throughout Brazil who were largely responsible for reviving Tim Maia's Rational recordings, buying the bootleg CDs and turning their friends on to this music along with other previously overlooked Brazilian cult classics that David remembers being exposed to during the same era: *A Tábua de Esmeralda* (Jorge Ben Jor, 1974), *Transa* (Caetano Veloso, 1972), *Todos Os Olhos* (Tom Zé, 1973), and *CARLOS, Erasmo . . .* (Erasmo Carlos, 1971).

Just as the US hip-hop scene from the late 1980s and early 1990s contributed to the domestic rediscovery of classic and rare soul, funk, disco, and anything with a break beat, the same thing was happening in São Paulo and Rio de Janeiro around the same time. While hip-hop crews definitely contributed to this trend, they weren't the only ones keeping Brazilian soul and funk alive. "In the early and mid-nineties there was a major phase of rediscovery for 'Samba Soul' and 'Samba Rock' movements thanks to local and international DJs that were really digging deep for very specific rare grooves," says Béco Dranoff, a New York City–based Brazilian expat and producer who curated and compiled the compilations *Samba Soul 70* (Ziriguiboom, 2001) and *Everything Is Possible: The Best of Os Mutantes* (Luaka Bop, 1999), as well as producing Bebel Gilberto's acclaimed 2000 international breakthrough album. "The old downtown Samba Rock parties became the cool places to be and with this buzz came the resurgence of the music of Tim, Bebeto, Hyldon, Cassiano, Gerson King Combo, Branca Di Neve, Banda Black Rio and many more."

Considered a novelty sound for most of the 1980s, hip-hop in Brazil had a small, devoted underground following, but mostly ignored by the major labels. The country's urban youth and some of its musicians embraced hip-hop instantaneously. Within a year of Sugarhill Gang's international hit, "Rapper's Delight," Brazil already had multiple cover versions, one with jazzy overtones and another with samba elements, naturally. Brazil's first generation of iconic hip-hop crews like Racionais MCs and Planet Hemp saw the connection between their North American hip-hop idols and their own domestic funk roots. While discussing how he came up with a name for their nascent crew, Mano Brown, founding member of influential São Paulo hip-hop crew Racionais MCs, said:

> Our inspiration came from North American [hip hop] groups, it's clear, because for our generation, rap was inspired by North American groups. We needed a name that would make it clear we're not a copy [of North American hip hop] and one day, I thought of Tim Maia, a Tim Maia record, *Tim Maia Racional*. I was on the bus and when I got to work I told Kleber, our DJ, "what about Racionais?"[6]

The name stuck and Brazil's equivalent to Public Enemy was born, giving a nod like P. E. did with their name, borrowed from their formative musical forefather, James Brown, and his 1972 single, "Public Enemy, Parts 1 & 2."

Mauricio Fleury, current keyboard and guitar player for Gal Costa as well as his own band Bixiga 70, remembers first hearing about Tim Maia's Rational records from Marcelo D2's first record from 1998 (lyrics at the beginning of this chapter). The former front man of Rio de Janeiro's founding hip-hop group, Planet Hemp, Marcelo D2 even performed a Tim Maia Racional song at an underground show in São Paulo in 1998.[7] Brazilian hip-hop sample spotters and lyrical investigators quickly picked up the clues these MCs and DJs encoded into their Brazilian beats, sparking a frenzy around these records. David remembers getting the Tim Maia Rational songs on an MP3 CD from a friend, never seeing the album artwork and not even knowing these songs originally came from two separate albums. "It was very unique, I had not heard anything like it from Brazil," David Galasse remembers upon hearing the Tim Maia Rational recordings for the first time. "Nothing in terms of groove and funk had ever come close to that. Tim Maia's voice seemed much more powerful, cleaner. Everything was intense. The arrangements reminded me a little of Stevie Wonder, but there were lots of Brazilian references there too. Ironic though it was, the songs went perfectly with all the drugs we used at the time."

For as many records as James Brown sold back in the day, his LPs are nearly impossible to find at most record stores around the United States and if you do find one, it's almost certainly whipped, most resembling a dog's well-loved Frisbee. Béco Dranoff confirms that the same was true of Tim's records in Brazil in the 1990s:

If you found them they would be in very bad shape. Suddenly the small soul and hip hop stores at São Paulo's Galeria do Rock started to sell bootleg CD compilations and full albums of these very rare gems. I bought a *Tim Maia Racional Vol. 1* on CD before it was officially reissued, and I was blown away. It was so groovy and perfect—it sounded like classic American R&B of the era, nothing like what was being released in Brazil.

"Many young people don't know his music from the seventies, which for me, and not just because I played on these songs, I think is a better phase, a more musical phase," Paulinho Guitarra says, going on to explain one of the roots of the Tim Maia Rational renaissance:

> At that time, the music press and the people hated these [Rational] albums. But in the eighties and nineties people started to rediscover them and listen to the albums again. Do you know where this started? In São Paulo in a shopping center called Galeria do Rock on São João Avenue. There they have lots of shops, little stalls, selling CDs, vinyl, rarities, etc. So, this album showed up there and somebody liked it and started to make copies and it turned into a cult thing. Nobody wanted it and then all of a sudden, the albums became more known and the price of the original vinyl went way up. And the new generation discovered him and started to listen to him in the era when he was doing "Me Dê Motivo" [a torchy, sentimental ballad and hit from 1983] and learned that he had cool stuff from before, soul music. It was really cool, this happened through the rediscovery of those albums. It became a new entry point for the next generation to Tim's seventies work.

These bizarre and mysterious recordings kick-started a slow and eventual reevaluation of Tim Maia's career, his catalog, and the historical impact extended to related artists and scenes as Brazilian academic Carlos Palombini writes:

The end of the millennium saw a rebirth of interest in *música soul* (a phrase that, in Brazilian parlance, may also encompass African-American funk, so as to distinguish it from the less prestigious *carioca* brand), to some extent due to the emergence in the media of issues related to racism and affirmative action policies. Since that point, new artists have appeared, old ones have returned and the careers of others who never stopped performing have received a new lease on life.[8]

In 1989, on the eve of the 1990s, Brazilian music beyond bossa nova finally made a splash stateside and with gusto in the UK. David Byrne, former front man of Talking Heads, launched a record label he called Luaka Bop to release, essentially, a "mix tape" of his favorite songs from records he picked up during various trips to Brazil. In the UK reissue labels Mr. Bongo, Soul Jazz, Strut, Whatmusic, and Far Out mined the record bins and record label archives to turn on new listeners to the likes of Marcos Valle, Joyce, and Azymuth. In Brazil, the newly available CD-burning technology helped spread this music, albeit illegally, to many more listeners. "Of course, it was from my actions that things spread," São Paulo record collector and dealer Rodrigo Piza explains, "but it was precisely at a time when technology began to democratize music in a very intense way." He acknowledges that he was likely the very first person to convert *Tim Maia Racional* from LP to a CD, but he never intended, nor benefited financially from the eventual widespread dissemination of the recordings, "I really had very little to do with it."

I collected rare records and I knew a kid who was burning CDs from LPs (a super new thing at the time, the end of the nineties), so I decided to try it out. I started with a few rock records and after I thought about *Tim Maia Racional*. The truth is I made it for myself and to give to some friends who would ask me for a copy. I never had the intention of selling them, but in the end, I sold some copies, very few in truth, about thirty at most, after which I stopped because the demand was growing, and I was worried there might be problems.

The demand for the pirated CDs spread like wildfire across multiple São Paulo demographics: teens, young adults, rockers, hip-hop kids, samba-rock dancers, and older Tim Maia fans who could finally listen to these albums they'd heard whispers about for so many years. With Rodrigo retiring after getting the ball rolling, it was open season on Tim Maia bootlegging in the hive-like Galeria do Rock with countless entrepreneurs getting in on the much easier process of making CD duplicates of one of Piza's originals. Having perused a good number of my Brazilian friends' and their friends' CD collections in Rio and São Paulo, my statistically insignificant research leads me to conclude that it's just as common to find a photocopied *Tim Maia Racional* CD as official issues of Jorge Ben Jor *A Tábua Esmeralda* or Gilberto Gil's *Refazenda* alongside samba, bossa nova, and 1980s and 1990s Brazilian rock. Friends Pedro and Camila, who I stayed with while in São Paulo during my research trip for this book, had two different bootleg copies, one very homemade-looking and the second compiling both Rational albums and clearly made professionally, despite its illegitimacy. "Until the end of the 90s, the general public didn't know of the existence of these records, they circulated only between retro DJs and collectors," Rodrigo says, "but with the rise of CD-Rs the possibility of making homemade copies, it started to circulate and became popular among middle class DJs, journalists and later the general public got in on it."

In 2002, the Brazilian film about Rio de Janeiro slum life and drug trafficking, *Cidade De Deus (City of God)*, featured Tim Maia's "O Caminho Do Bem" playing over the film's end credits. This would be the first official release of any Tim Maia Rational song since *Tim Maia Racional* Vol. 2 was originally released door-to-door in 1975. *Tim Maia Racional* Vol. 1 finally saw an official reissue on CD in 2006 thanks to Trama, an independent Brazilian record label, releasing the album remastered and as well as in a version ripped directly from the LP, preserving the nostalgic pops and clicks of the previous bootleg for the generation of Brazilians who grew up on the imperfect CD-Rs. Evidently, Trama ran out of steam as a business before it could release *Tim Maia Racional* Vol. 2 as planned, but that's where Luaka Bop came into the picture with their 2012 release, *World Psychedelic Classics, Volume 4: The Existential Soul of Tim Maia: Nobody Can Live Forever,* which included six songs from the two Rational albums and twelve of the fifteen tracks chosen for the compilation were recorded during Tim's Seroma phase, emerging from the shed on Vitória Régia Street overlooking the Rodrigo de Freitas Lagoon.

Interlude: Carmelo, Tell Me What to Do

Knowing about some of the ongoing legal issues connected to the Rational records, I reached out to Carmelo Maia by email very early during my research for this book. I informed him of my plans to write this book and ask whether he'd be available for an interview. I had every intention of interviewing him and giving him all the respect, I gave anyone else I interviewed for this project, but he declined, or rather, his lawyer did.

Aside from complaints about how and where Tim's music is being licensed, the chief offense leveled at Carmelo Maia is for licensing Seroma tracks recorded by his father that were written alongside Tim's bandmates or entirely by bandmates or friends of Tim's and not paying the actual songwriters anything. It all started with the track "O Caminho Do Bem," which Carmelo licensed for the film *Cidade De Deus* (*City of God*). Thanks to the film's international success, Tim Maia's Rational recordings reached millions of new ears around the world. According to the rare insert that came with the original Seroma LP of *Tim Maia Racional* Vol. 2, the song was composed by Beto Cajueiro, Paulinho Guitarra, and Serginho Trombone, and while Tim helped (as described earlier) fitting the Rational Culture scripture to the deeply funky groove, he's not credited as one of the three songwriters. A conflict over the rights to the songs controlled by Carmelo but claimed by Paulinho has now escalated to the point of legal action as Paulinho is seeking royalties for these songs controlled by Seroma, which Carmelo controls as part of Tim's estate. Though they might be extremely rare, the paper inserts found in the original releases of the Rational and albums demonstrate, irrefutably, who originally wrote these songs.

Paulinho, along with Don Pi, Fábio, and the estates of Beto Cajueiro and Robson Jorge are owed money for songs Tim recorded that have been subsequently licensed for use or reissue by Carmelo Maia. The wife of Paulinho Guitarra and a lawyer by training, Jane Lapa, attests that Carmelo forged Paulinho's signature in order to cheat his own godfather (that's right, Carmelo is Paulinho's godson) out of his writing credit on "O Caminho Do Bem." Paulinho continues to wage a legal battle with Carmelo over his songs, but even more so, over his identity, as he's been completely frozen out of anything related to Tim Maia, except for *Tim Maia Racional* Vol. 3, only thanks to Kassin's insistence and clout.

"Carmelo knew Tim very little," Hyldon told the *A Folha de São Paulo*'s Emmanuel Bonfim. "He was raised by his aunt and grandmother. The guy is not worried about his father's legacy. Gee, you hear Tim's music in the grocery store! Whatever money he's offered, he licenses Tim's music. He's even changed some of the lyrics [of Tim's songs], you know? Historical songs! I warned him here at my home: 'After I die, if you license my songs to the supermarket, I'll come back here,'" Hyldon joked about the few songs from Tim's publishing company that he wrote or co-wrote.[1]

Carlos Cajueiro, son of Tim's bassist and close friend Beto Cajueiro, posted a scathing critique of the *Tim Maia* biopic on Facebook shortly after its release, starting a firestorm of comments, and even Carmelo entered the fray. "Carmelo, along with journalist Nelson Motta, denied the true story of his legitimate mother!" Carlos complained, referring to the fictional love interest, "Janaina," invented for the film instead of basing the character on Carmelo's actual mother, Geisa, or Tim's prior steady girlfriend, Janete. He went on to add, referring to his father's writing credits, "Carmelo is dishonestly managing Tim's songs, not paying the copyright to the true composers of many of Tim Maia's songs."[2]

Carmelo's response to Carlos was transparent but failed to address Carlos' (and Paulinho's) complaints, "Cajueiro, the legal process is easy, if you get to know me, come to my house, come and experience the 400 lawsuits I have inherited, come sit down and talk with good intentions and understand this whole universe called Tim Maia."

I have no doubt that the Tim Maia estate that Carmelo inherited at the age of twenty-three was an absolute mess. If Tim's health was in poor shape for lack of regular medical check-ups, you can imagine the equivalent neglect his financial affairs suffered. Being careless and a narcissist is a dangerous combination and Tim frequently took advantage of people's trust assuming Tim would pay; sometimes he did and sometimes he didn't. Sometimes the subterfuge was intentional and sometimes he just forgot. Carmelo Maia, as the sole legal heir of his father's estate, alongside a cadre of lawyers, had to make sense of everything. To his credit, he's successfully revived his father's legacy through a number of high profile projects, like the 2014 biopic, the earlier Broadway-style musical, and a number of official Tim Maia tribute projects.

Sadly, nearly all of the projects released to date about Tim's life, including Nelson and Fábio's books, the Tim Maia musical and 2014 film, focus more on Tim's pratfalls than his musical genius. Living the way he did with little regard for others' approval, fueled by jealousy and paranoia, especially during the coke-filled 1980s and early 1990s, Tim's exploits became the thing of urban legend: "Did you hear what Tim said on Jô Soares' show (Brazil's equivalent to Johnny Carson)?" In the decade and half before his death and the years since, he's as known for his antics as he is for his music. Beginning in the 1980s, the media coverage was more about him saying ridiculous things than about his music. Like Dave Chappelle's Rick James character, Tim Maia had devolved into a one-trick-pony, however entertaining that trick still was.

Carmelo Maia continues to reap the financial benefits of this tired joke made at his father's expense, while withholding royalties to some of Tim's oldest friends and the musicians, and in the case of Paulinho, excluding him from future projects related in any way to his father's music. "I just kept my father's command alive," Carmelo told *A Folha de Sao Paulo.* "Anyone who filed suit would never be a part of something of his or about him. Paulinho sued my father after he died. He will not be in any project of Tim Maia, just as he was not in the movie."[3] The 2014 film, in its attempt to cut Paulinho Guitarra and Don Pi out of the story, incorporates an ersatz band, apparently based on some photos of Tim's multi-racial hippie band of the early

1970s. Instead of including Tim's actual friends and bandmates in the story, the film fictionalizes and overstates Tim's friend Fábio's role, giving him Paulinho's part as bandleader. Fábio was certainly Tim's friend, but he was not a part of Tim's band during the 1970s as he had his own music career. Sure, liberties need to be taken in order to transform a book to the screen, but it would have been a lot easier, more respectful, and more interesting to just base the characters on the actual group: an early 1970s, fast-living, multi-racial, hippie funk band. "[There were] lots of lies in the film," Paulinho Trompete #1 says. "The film was poorly told and poorly made. I didn't like it and it felt disgusted seeing Tim acting weird; he wasn't like that."

"After the biopic and the contested version that aired on Rede Globo, Tim Maia will once again be honored. This time, on stage," writes Emmanuel Bonfim in *A Folha de São Paulo* in 2015 about a proposed tour celebrating Tim's repertoire.

> The Nivea Viva project, in its fourth edition, drew on *O Síndico's* (Building Manager) [Tim's nickname while living in the same apartment building with Jorge Ben Jor in the 1980s] powerful hits to sustain yet another tribute to one of Brazilian music's bigwigs. The faces of Tim's soul repertoire will be rapper Criolo and singer Ivete Sangalo. And the choice of these artists has already caused controversy.[4]

For those unfamiliar with the two contemporary Brazilian stars invited to interpret Tim's catalogue, it would be like choosing Mos Def and J-Lo.

11 The Rescue and Reconstruction of *Tim Maia Racional* Vol. 3

Just as Tim lived his life doing everything the hard way, so went the making of *Tim Maia Racional* Vol. 3. Only a handful of people knew about the existence of a rumored third volume of Rational recordings until 2007, when five songs appeared on a Brazilian blog, described as the lost Rational recordings, presumably recorded at the end of his time with Rational Culture.

In June 2016, I met with Kassin at his modest two-story townhouse studio off a bustling street in Botafogo, Rio de Janeiro, to talk about how he ended up with unreleased tapes of the holy grail of Brazilian soul and funk music. While not officially included within the purview of this book, *Tim Maia Racional* Vol. 3 is just as essential an artifact of Tim's time involved in Rational Culture as the first two albums. The story of the album's rescue from near-destruction to its reconstruction among a reunion of Tim Maia friends and family is symbolic of the continued complications that continue to shade Tim Maia's legacy.

For Kassin, the project was a labor of love. As a lifelong Tim Maia fan, he realized the opportunity to meet some of Tim's old bandmates, who he'd admired from a distance for as long as he can remember. Kassin is one of those rare music personalities that excels on many fronts: he's a great musician; a multi-instrumentalist; a fantastic, creative, in-demand producer; he's expressive, eloquent, and deeply knowledgeable about music, Brazilian and far beyond; and on top of all that, he's a really nice, easy-going Carioca. He's a self-proclaimed music nerd and doesn't hesitate to play the part with his big hair, an impressive mess of dark brown curls framing his thick-framed glasses.

> I am a Tim Maia fan, so I thought it was strange to have it [these unreleased Rational recordings] at my home and I can listen to this incredible piece of music and I wanted everyone else to have this right. I'm a music producer, you know, this kind of project you don't do for money. It's not my production, but it was a pain in the ass to make it happen. The music part was easy, like we did the whole thing in five days, all of Lincoln's [Olivetti] parts, all of Paulinho's [Guitarra] parts and the strings and the mix we did in four days. The thing is there already, I didn't do much. But the thing is, to make it happen legally, it was really, really hard.[1]

Kassin reflects on this project that took years to complete, beginning in 2006 when he was producing an album for ex-Tamba Trio bassist Bebeto Castilho where William Luna Jr. was working as an audio engineer. William's father, William Luna Sr., was the owner of two of Rio de Janeiro's few independent recording studios during the 1970s and 1980s, Hawaii and Somil. During these years, a majority of commercial music was recorded by the record companies in the recording studios they owned and operated, so independent studios mostly catered to other kinds of recording needs, like commercial jingles and soundtracks.

When Tim Maia was in search of a professional recording studio to finish his Rational vocals and overdubs after parting ways with RCA, Somil was just the place, close to his apartment in Copacabana and equipped with decent equipment, though a step down from RCA's state-of-the-art studio. As soon as Tim said his hurried goodbyes to Seu Manoel, he was no longer interested in anything to do with Rational Culture, so he presumably left the unfinished tapes there at the studios, where they hid in plain sight for decades.

While working for Tim Maia as one of his sound guys in the early 1990s, William Luna Jr. was helping his father consolidate the unclaimed tapes from the Somil studio, the studio's equivalent to a "dead letters office." Tapes were being transferred to William Sr.'s other studio, Hawaii, except for the few for which the technology to transfer them to another format was no longer available. One of these one-inch tapes stood out to William Luna Jr. "These tapes caught my attention, I don't know why, maybe because 'Tim Maia' was written on them," William Jr. says during our interview that took place, coincidentally, in the old RCA studios where Tim and band recorded the backing tracks for the original Rational albums. "I held on to them for a long time. I was already working with Tim at the time, but I never brought them up with Tim because he didn't like to talk about these years. He didn't like a lot of things," William Jr. recalls, explaining why he never bothered to ask Tim about these tapes. William remembers Tim hated red-colored shirts and AKG 414 microphones (evidently, because it was the same microphone he used recording backup vocals for Erasmo Carlos), so "to talk about these tapes, would be to end my working relationship with Tim."[2]

"I started to hear stories about Tim's missing recordings and thought these could be them and that's when I took them to Kassin," William Jr. explains, though he left out the part of the story where he gave the tape to another Tim Maia fan, a São Paulo record collector named Dudu Marote. The recordings remained a secret for a few years, until William passed them to Kassin who tried to negotiate an official release for the recordings. On the eve of announcing the official release of *Tim Maia Racional* Vol. 3 with Kassin as the producer, a version of the tapes with five songs found their way onto a Brazilian music blog.

I remember when these raw recordings dropped; they were a revelation. It was almost unbelievable, and at first I was a bit incredulous, but then upon listening to the clearly unfinished tracks more closely, they were unmistakably Tim Maia, unfinished, but authentic. Marote might not have known it at the time, but the versions he possessed, which were the same versions found online, were missing two of the eight multitracked parts originally recorded by Tim Maia, because when William Jr. first transferred the tapes neither of them knew at the time that the machine wasn't working properly, and it failed to transfer two of the instrumental tracks. Later, while working with Kassin, William Jr. did another transfer after fixing the machine and retrieved the Tim Maia recordings in their entirety as well as identifying one more song, to make six new Rational recordings.

Kassin started reaching out to Tim's estate to try to coordinate a release, but his phone calls to Carmelo Maia's lawyer went unanswered. Fortuitously, Nelson Motta reached out to Kassin around this time to book one of Kassin's musical projects,

Orquestra Imperial, to play his Tim Maia book launch party. After discussing the details of the party with Tim's old friend, Kassin played him the unknown tracks, hoping he could enlist Nelson to move the project along. After picking up the pieces of his brain that had exploded all over his apartment, Nelson agreed to reach out to the Tim Maia family, "which was really important because he had the trust of the family and the lawyers," Kassin explains.

Finally, with critical assistance from Flávio Pinheiro, who managed Sony's back catalog, a deal with the massive newspaper and magazine publisher Abril was inked to include *Tim Maia Racional* Vol. 3 as the bonus disc in the already planned Tim Maia box set slated for release in 2012. This box set would also contain the first ever reissue of *Tim Maia Racional* Vol. 2 on CD. Now, with a modest budget in place and plan for release, Kassin set to work to complete the album that Tim and band left unfinished back in 1975.

"I didn't feel it was my right to finish the record without having his original gang together," Kassin explains about his decision to invite only musicians who had previously worked with Tim to help complete the album, like Paulinho Guitarra, Serginho Trombone, Chiquinho (from Tim's 1980s band), and Lincoln Olivetti, who worked extensively with Tim Maia beginning shortly after the Rational phase. At the beginning of the process Kassin didn't know that he would need to rerecord certain parts like Paulinho Guitarra's guitar and Don Pi's keyboard that Tim had condensed along with the backup vocals by Terezinha and Elza to one track in order to make room on the tape for the strings. "I had to redo the stacked tracks because the tracking was off, and the tuning was fucked up and it was impossible to fix," Kassin remembers. Don Pi was in Germany and couldn't participate in the sessions, so Kassin asked Lincoln to replay those parts and Paulinho Guitarra redid his parts. Beyond replaying his own parts, Paulinho's major contribution to this project was his historical memory. Kassin only had the tapes, no studio notes, no song titles or even authors, he recalls; "I didn't know who wrote them, but Paulinho remembered, he remembered everything, he took notes, he had a diary, so it was impossible to make this thing properly, like I wanted to do, without Paulinho. There was no way." Something as seemingly simple as finding out who played drums on these recordings, Paulinho came to the rescue. "I was certain it was that guy . . . Paulinho [Batera], when he does a drum fill or solo he makes a whining sound, and it [whining] showed up on the tapes and nobody knew who this guy was."

However, Paulinho Guitarra's participation nearly derailed the whole project. On one of the final days of recording the strings and finishing the project, Tim's son Carmelo dropped by the studio where Kassin was working with Lincoln Olivetti, Serginho Trombone, and a whole string section hired to play Lincoln's arrangements. Most of these guys were old friends and many of them knew Carmelo since he was a baby, so the atmosphere was really chummy; that is, until "Paulinho arrived, and right away they started arguing and there was a huge fight, screaming at each other and Carmelo was like, 'if he's a part of this project, the project stops now!'" Kassin responded, "this project is only happening if he's a part of it, there's no way to make it happen without him. He's part of this music, there's no way to do it without him." Kassin remembers the air in the cozy production booth was almost solid while the string players (out in the studio) were holding their breath, until Kassin and others could calm Carmelo down enough for him to agree to allow the project to proceed.

Kassin personally knew some of these musicians, like Paulinho Guitarra, before starting this project, but another, Lincoln Olivetti, he'd never met, though Kassin considered him a personal idol. Olivetti, who passed away in 2015, was best known as a producer and arranger, though he was also a gifted keyboard player and songwriter. Kassin called him in to play the missing keyboard parts that needed re-recording, but also to add the missing string arrangements. Not wanting to piss him off but aiming for perfection on the *Racional* Vol. 3 project, Kassin gingerly approached Lincoln about how he wanted the maestro to score these songs. "I don't want you to do your thing, I want you to do what would be a Rational arrangement," Kassin told his hero, nervously. "Look, you normally do these kinds of harmonies [Kassin demonstrates], and you can't do that because they only have these kinds of harmonies on Tim Maia records *after* you arrived, two years later. You cannot use these kinds of chords, everything should be like triads and you know like, old stuff. Don't think the way you think, think like it was before." Not only did Lincoln appreciate Kassin's advice, because he admitted he wouldn't have thought about it in that way, but Kassin's directness and clear passion for Tim's legacy impressed the notoriously icy Lincoln, kick-starting a friendship that lasted until Olivetti passed and beyond, as Kassin has a new, all-too-familiar struggle, this time with the Olivetti estate, trying to release a posthumous Lincoln Olivetti solo project.

The six-song release delivers twenty-nine minutes of fresh rational recordings, five of the songs previously unreleased, as well as a new version of "Que Legal," which originally appeared on *Racional* Vol. 2. The album opens with "É Preciso Ler e Reler" (Its Necessary to Read and Reread), a mystical ballad, draped in warm strings and surrounded by reassuring congas, that dance around the beat as Tim sings about "bathing in rational energy." Paulinho's guitar darts in and out of the proceedings, dodging the strings as they swoop in over Lincoln's elegant piano figures. This tune of Tim's is arguably the classiest of all of the Rational recordings, mostly thanks to Paulinho's delicate guitar work and the beautiful string arrangement Lincoln Olivetti composed decades later to complete the song.

On *Racional* Vol. 3 Tim makes up for not including an English-language song on *Racional* Vol. 2, the first album to not include a song in soul music's mother tongue since he started his recording career. "I Am Rational" is another Tim Maia composition, like "Guinéa Bissau, Moçambique e Angola," where the funk is evident in the pauses, the stretching of horn lines, and the spaces between guitar wah-wahs. Lyrically, Tim borrows a trick from "Que Legal," ditching the insider-baseball Rational Culture-ese in favor of English vernacular that explains, "I don't need no dope, I am rational . . . and when you read the book, *Universe in Disenchantment*, you won't need no dope, you're gonna be Rational." Locking into a monster groove, Tim and company milk it for over five minutes, trading off fuzzy guitar solos, brass bursts, and funky drum breaks, while Tim repeats the above English-language Rational mantra.

During my interview with Paulinho Guitarra, he points at a photo of bassist Valdecir Nei Machado:

He was the best and baddest bass player. He was [later] in Banda Black Rio. He was in Apocalypse Band and we became friends and then when Tim was looking for a bass player, I told him, "I have Willie Weeks here in Niterói!"[3] There's a song on *Racional* Vol. 3 that I wrote the words and music to ["Lendo O Livro" (Reading the Book)] and he's the bassist, [playing] just like Willie Weeks!

"Lendo O Livro" leaps out of the starting blocks like a classic Motown rave-up with a jangly tambourine urging Valdecir's bubbling bass line toward the finish line as Tim sings Paulinho's words: "For a long time, everyone's been looking for a solution to the suffering that's caused by illusion in thinking." Lincoln's strings complete the Motown-esque composition. Throughout *Racional* Vol. 3 Lincoln's arrangements are impeccable, perfectly recreating a mid-1970s soul music backdrop, "not his typical, hysterical style, but instead something with more of a sixties vibe, like Billy Strange or Jack Nitzsche," Kassin says.

Sitting in Kassin's Botafogo studio listening to Lincoln's isolated strings, then Tim's vocals from the Rational ballad "O Supermundo Racional" (The Rational Superworld), I have to imagine Tim would be happy to know his old friends and musicians were completing this beautiful and crazy music. Soloing Tim's vocals, they send a chill down my spine, so strong, confident, and emotional. Kassin mentions that among all the tracks on the original tape, the vocals tracks were "in perfect condition," already doubled-up and with the reverb perfectly placed, adding rhetorically, "he was singing incredibly, no?" On tracks like this one, it's difficult to imagine Tim's original vision, as so much of the track's dynamism comes from Lincoln's tasteful, latter-day arrangement that beautifully tee-up Tim's Rational words:

Todos vão voltar (Everyone will return)

Seu estado natural (To your natural state)

Vamos regressar (Let's go back)

Pro supermundo Racional (To the Rational Superworld)

Como era antes disso aqui descer (Like it was before this happened here)

Como era antes disso aqui descer (Like it was before this happened here)

The lyrics to the next song, "Nação Cósmica" (Cosmic Nation) read like a speech, dense and unmusical, but set to a hyperactive funk track frequently pierced by razor-sharp horn stabs; the perfect soundtrack for a high-speed car-chase scene. "Brazil is already considered a cosmic nation for having birthed in Brazil the knowledge to prepare humanity to enter in contact with our true world of origin, the Rational Superworld," start the cosmic and strangely patriotic lyrics. Musically building and releasing like fellow-Brasileiro Eumir Deodato's jazz-funk cover of "Also Sprach Zarathustra" (the theme to *2001*), "Nação Cósmica" grooves like a mother for almost six-and-a-half minutes, completely immune to the dry-as-dirt "lyrics" delivered in his preacher, talk-sing style with occasional breaks for Paulinho's red-hot guitar solos. Four-and-a-half minutes deep, Tim finishes his speech repeating the old chestnut from the first two volumes, "I had to climb, up there on high, to see . . . Rational energy, the true light of humanity," before his horn section alternates licks for the final minute and half over the same double-time drum and percussion track.

The final track on Tim's posthumous Rational release is a re-recording of the track "Que Legal," which appeared first on *Racional* Vol. 2. Not dissimilar from the radical reimagining of "Que Beleza" between the first and second Rational albums, Tim delivers this version of "Que Legal" in a slowed-down tempo with a totally different arrangement, while still retaining a strong Latin vibe. Recognizing that the song was not new, and the arrangement still unfinished, Kassin and Lincoln tried something unconventional in order to give the song a different feel. "It was a kind of liberty we took," Kassin says referring to Lincoln's suggestion of using a Moog keyboard (an instrument Tim and band were not known for employing) to play some bass parts, which gives the song a buzzing low-end. Kassin remembers, "Everyone in the studio agreed—it should be different than the other one."

Conclusion: Tim Maia, A Man in Search of Answers

He was a person with his own defects, but deep down he was a good person. He called me one New Year's Eve to come party with him and at four in the morning we went to the beach giving away good amounts of money to the people cleaning up the trash on the beach. "Paulinho, I want you to ask the guys how many children they have. If they have three kids, I want you to give them 300 reais, if it's ten kids, that's 1,000 reais," and so we must have given away 10,000 reias, me and Tim with a bottle of whiskey between us, drinking and giving away money. He really liked helping people who didn't have anything. But the film doesn't talk about this side of him.

PAULINHO TROMPETE #1 (PAULO ROBERTO DE OLIVEIRA)

"Tim was a very lonely person at the end of the day," Don Pi says about his old friend. "He had a heavy temper and he suffered a lot when he broke up with his girlfriend," not to mention when he felt disrespected or cheated. Restless and lonely, Tim sought solace at the bottom of Chivas bottles and countless joints in a twenty-four-hour party atmosphere. "My impression as a seventeen-year-old boy lead me to feel that all that, it was just too much," Don Pi remembers of when he first met Tim right before his Rational Culture chapter. "Too many drugs, too much alcohol, too much weed and everything all at the same time. I thought, one day somebody's gonna die here, and thank god that never happened." It's possible to argue that his year-and-a-half reprieve from the rock n' roll lifestyle saved Tim, but whatever health benefits gained during his Rational phase were immediately squandered, snorted, guzzled, and engorged in the aftermath of his departure from Rational Culture, but this regression also fueled the fantastic recordings that followed. Paulinho Guitarra acknowledges that Tim Maia was certainly an alcoholic, but beyond that he doesn't agree with the biopic director's theory (from the book's introduction, page 14) that Tim unconsciously was looking to police himself:

> Tim didn't have a problem . . . what was his problem? Women, because he was very jealous . . . like the Donny Hathaway song,[1] he was a jealous guy. I think his problem was whiskey and [sucking sound mimicking smoking a joint], which is not really a problem. He wanted to try something different and then he was abducted, seduced by Manoel Jacintho Coelho. He didn't go to Rational Culture to change his life. It was his curiosity; he thought it was a really cool thing.

Nelson Motta once said, "Tim Maia is one of the smartest people I know. He's a master of improvisation and a born comedian,"[2] but like that crab with the one oversized claw, Tim's puny claw represented his insecurities, jealousy, and mistrust of even his closest compatriots. Paulinho Martins, a.k.a. Paulinho Trompete #2, was not the only person I interviewed who referred to Tim as *"criança adulto"* (adult child). "He had the mentality of a child; he'd see things this way and thought it was totally normal." He recounts this story from the early 1970s in São Paulo as they're about to play a show. Tim convened a rehearsal in his hotel room "with all of the instruments: the drummer hitting the table, everybody plugged-in and the horns playing in the room. He noticed through the window, there was a music instrument store across the street and says, 'hey, Paulinho Guitarra, go down there and ask the guy to let us borrow some instruments.'" The faithful, but realistic sidekick tried everything he could think of to say except for "no." "Tell him it's for Tim Maia," but Paulinho Guitarra stood his ground against his overgrown kid boss. "Tim, they're not gonna do it, forget it man."

True to the cliché, Tim was his own worst enemy. Ruy Castro, the Brazilian music journalist who interviewed him for Brazil's *Playboy* magazine in 1991, wrote: "Behind this effervescence, there is a person almost naive, who could have had even more power than he boasted of, and others who are much less talented—and smarter—have done better. No one is able to stop Tim Maia from being himself, not even him."[3] Even though he's gone, Tim's legacy continues to exhibit the same qualities he was known for in life: unpredictability, nonconformity, and controversy, but sadly his music is often missing from the discussion.

Where I once thought of Tim's Rational albums as historical aberrations in his discography, which they certainly are lyrically, I can now see them as the centerpieces of Tim Maia's most prolific and artistically free phase, the Seroma years from 1973 to 1977. The body of work Tim recorded and released during these years stands out for two reasons: Tim's lyrical intensity and the Seroma Band's cohesion. To tell the story of the music, you need to tell the story of the musicians. If this book accomplishes anything, I hope it gives credit where credit is long overdue to the pioneering musicians who played music with Tim, who partied with Tim, and the proud few who even followed their hero into an extraterrestrial-obsessed cult. Tim and his bandmates radically reimagined Afro-Brazilian cultural identities throughout the 1970s, first with his introduction of soul music to Brazil and then later in his recasting himself as an independent, black artist with his own motherfucking band! "What he wanted was a band that was like a troop, a team that travels the world together," Paulinho Guitarra remembers.

Over the course of four-and-a-half years (1973–7) Tim recorded six albums and a single with a tight knit crew of musicians, anchored by Paulinho Guitarra. "On previous records, we would rehearse as a band and then when we went into the studio there would be other musicians," Paulinho Trompete #2 says, having recorded on some of Tim's earliest sessions before he started producing his own records, "but for these records we were really united, for nearly two years playing together almost every day." Paulinho Trompete #1 agrees, "The union of the group was really important, because at the time there were only *baile* bands that played live shows, there weren't any bands working directly with a singer like Tim Maia. I don't have any bad memories of that time. I learned a lot from Tim. And he really appreciated his band's loyalty."

As a black man in the Brazilian recording industry, Tim Maia was a trailblazer in his work from the control booth, playing a major role in the production of his records (since 1974) not to mention his pioneering role in the independent music scene. Paulinho Trompete #2 (Paulinho Martins) recalls his ability to single-handedly mastermind a recording session:

> Tim was a spectacle. He was one of Brazil's greatest artists ever. Everything he composed was a hit. He was a genius. "We're gonna record tomorrow! We'll make the arrangements when we get there." And when we got there, he started with the bass, dictating all the parts, one by one, and then yelling to the engineering booth, "Let's record!"

Necessity being the mother of invention, Tim learned how to do things in the music business in order to circumvent the establishment wherever he could. Beyond their bizarreness, Tim Maia's Rational records are significant as the very first independent releases in Brazil by a mainstream artist. Lula Côrtez and Ze Ramalho's legendary northeastern holy grail *Paêbirú*, from 1975, is often cited as a first, but *Tim Maia Racional* was also released in 1975 (almost certainly earlier in the year) and unlike Lula and Zé, Tim was one of the biggest pop stars in Brazil at the time of its release. Thirty-eight thousand records (for the first album) is no small amount to produce and distribute without previous experience. The guy who's usually credited with inventing the independent recording industry in Brazil with his classic pop-fusion-jazz record from 1977, *Feito Em Casa* (Home Made), is Antonio Adolfo, but even he credits Tim for a lot of what he gets credit for. "Tim Maia gave me lots of tips about how to do this, how to do that, a list of all the stores that would buy my albums, because he'd done this with the group from Seu Manoel," Antonio says during a phone interview from July 2017. "He was very helpful . . . but he was crazy, because once my album became famous through the press, he said to me, 'Oh, Antonio, you didn't acknowledge me after I gave you all that information.' Tim Maia was like that. He was a great friend, a close friend."[4]

Tim's path to success was never easy, challenging the mainstream Brazilian media that at times denigrated his music as a carbon-copy of American soul music, accusing him of importing foreign styles that didn't belong (meanwhile Brazilian art rockers Novos Baianos, Milton Nascimento, and Caetano Veloso were heralded as the future of Brazilian pop music). The Brazilian recording industry historically pushed artists that fit nicely into an unobjectionable, middle-class worldview like the Bahian mafia of Caetano Veloso, Gilberto Gil, Maria Bethânia, and Gal Costa, whose peaceful, intellectual, macrobiotic agenda was inoffensive and even self-congratulatory to the majority white cultural elites and record label honchos. "Gil and Caetano—it's a religion that remains in Brazil until today," Ed Motta says about how certain artists were promoted over others. "It's like they are the only ones who the press puts on the covers and anything they talk about is the only thing that matters." Ed singles out the guy who signed Tim Maia (president of Philips Records, André Midani) as one of the architects of this marketing of Brazil's greatest export since bossa nova. "He invented these things. The *Tropicália* thing was Midani."

What came after *Tropicália* was even more exclusive in its own nebulous way: M.P.B., an abbreviation of *Música Popular Brasileira*, which means everything, and nothing, depending on what the record labels decided to promote. Tim nailed it, back in 1983, in conversation with Jamari França: "There is a disgraceful intellectuality in the artistic medium. . . . It says it doesn't like American [influences] and it's the most influenced [by North American music] since Pixinguinha's time. *Música Popular Brasileira*? There is no such thing, there is no M.P.C., Chinese popular music, or M.P.A., American popular music, it's just a label."[5] Just a year earlier, in conversation with Tárik de Souza, Tim makes his point, as usual in the most extreme possible way, by tearing down all that is sacred in Brazilian culture:

> *Chorinho* is not Brazilian culture, it is a mixture of fado with tango. *Samba de Breque*[6] is Argentinian slang; the *malandro* did not exist in Brazil. The Brazilian is mestizo and every mestizo is crazy, I know that, because I breed dogs. If it's pure-bred, then all right, but if it's mixed, its gonna be crazy. . . . In the United States they washed the Negro culturally to become white. Not here, they just beat the shit out of him, hit him with a stick, and the more they hit him, the more he would beat the drum.[7]

Tim Maia was punk and hip-hop, ten years too soon: uninvited, infectious, irresistible, and offensive to the ruling class. The point that he so crudely overstates is that everything that the critics and cultural elites hold sacred is a hybrid, a mix. From *chorinho* to bossa nova and on to *Jovem Guarda*, Tropicália (at least it had its own manifesto) and M.P.B., what Tim and his crew (Hyldon, Cassiano, Banda Black Rio, Sandra Sá, Carlos Dafé, Lincoln Olivetti and Robson Jorge) created starting in the late 1960s and going strong through the early 1980s was no different, a hybrid, beautiful and unique and no less Brazilian than the classic recordings of Jorge Ben Jor, Caetano Veloso, Gilberto Gil, João Gilberto, and Tom Jobim.

The topic of the 2014 biopic about Tim came up while I was interviewing musician and arranger Laercio de Freitas and his daughter Thalma de Freitas backstage while she finished doing her make-up for the show starting ten minutes later. Thalma is a singer, performer, and a former Brazilian telenovela star, who now lives in Los Angeles. As I was interviewing her father about Tim Maia's legacy, she couldn't help but interject:

> The movie is made for White, rich people from Brazil; it's their narrative, the cultural elite's perspective. But you're talking about a Black man from Brazil, the *periferia* (lower class suburbs) of Brazil, who was born poor, but extremely smart and talented. So, over the course of his life he became extremely sarcastic and bitter. He was fucking up everything because he was fucking-up the fuckers that were fucking him! "He was so exotic, he was so eccentric, he was so crazy"—he was a Black man, you can't take that out of the equation.[8]

In his 1982 story about Tim in *Jornal do Brasil*, Tárik de Souza observed:

> Such musical objectivity, full of undeniable talent, is the only thing to explain the survival of this [approach] opposite to the artistic pattern in the market. Committed to demoralizing the industry's records, he attributes the sales crisis [at the time of this article] in part to "fabricated and sustained stars with exorbitant payola," which he accuses the record companies of continuing to pay.[9]

Among the many challenges Tim and his music faced and continues to face are the tyranny of lyrics over music. Brazilian rocker Eduardo Araújo remembers Tim saying, "It's more important to have swing than the right lyrics."[10] While Bob Dylan gets a pass for (mostly) predictable and uninventive music, James Brown's lyrics relegate his legacy to a less-serious status. Rodrigo Piza, the Galeria do Rock record vendor, explains this Brazilian and global double standard:

> Tim was (and perhaps still is) not seen as an M.P.B. great. I believe it is because of his lyrics, because in Brazil they weigh the lyrics sometimes more than the music. So, when it comes to Chico Buarque, for example, the words are emphasized much more than the melody, energy, or historical popularity. In the case of Tim's lyrics like "Eu Amo Você Menina" (I Love You Girl) or "Gostava Tanto de Você" (I Liked You So Much) and many others, perhaps they were not considered to be serious enough. Certainly, it has changed a little. Now, I think he is considered a more serious artist and is more widely respected because the quality of his music spoke louder.[11]

Of course, Tim Maia had words for Chico Buarque and his high-brow, poetic, and sophisticated sambas: "Chico Buarque is always saying this thing, that musicality is limited, but he has freaked out on a lot of people; he has even started a school for people freaking out about Brazilian music."[12] The snubs and rejections from the M.P.B. establishment and the domestic recording industry didn't stop Tim. In 1983, Jamari França wrote:

These problems all upset Tim Maia even though he was accustomed to the harshness he faced in his life and included prison passages for stealing a chair and smoking marijuana before he was famous, and six years of living in the United States where he did everything, even working as a mortician, living in a thousand different places, sleeping on the street and doing his hustles.[13]

Ironically, the lyrics from a couple of Tim's Rational songs were the first to elevate Tim's lyrical game. The lyrics to "Bom Senso" and "Que Beleza" showcase universal, adult themes, hinting that Tim was open to writing about and exploring ideas beyond the simple love song tropes that most of his previous and later hits were built on. Interestingly, his English-language songs from the Seroma phase carried much of the lyrical weight with songs like "Nobody Can Live Forever," "Brother Father Sister Mother," and "Let's Have a Ball Tonight" providing a view to an artist exploring new ideas and ways of communicating with his audience. Brazilian pop music of the late 1960s and 1970s doesn't have the same tradition of message-songs, overtly political songs like you had in the United States with "What's Goin' On" or "For What It's Worth," primarily because of the military dictatorship that forced lyricists to camouflage their critiques in increasingly subtle and ingenious ways. While Chico Buarque, Caetano Veloso, Tom Zé, and others have been celebrated and documented for their cleverly subversive lyrics, Tim's deep Seroma-era lyrics raised few eyebrows, those of censors, critics, or Tim Maia fans, his fresh social commentary likely getting lost in the mess of far-out ideas Tim introduced during this phase.

Regardless of what the critics and elites think of Tim Maia and his lyrics, his music continues to excite Brazilians of all ages and the revolution he started when he introduced soul and funk to Brazil continues to reverberate throughout Brazil and beyond. A quick survey of the influences and roots of modern Afro-Brazilian music, from Brazilian soul descendants to Brazilian hip-hop and *baile funk* artists, concludes that all threads lead back to Tim Maia and the dozens of musicians he mentored, many of whom went on to make major contributions to Brazilian music for subsequent decades. "Tim's music was fundamental to opening the doors for the Black pride movement that took roots in Brazilian music. It's interesting to think that before him, soul music was not such a part of the Brazilian sonic kaleidoscope and now it is a key ingredient," Béco Dranoff says. "Tim's music helped solidify the samba soul and hip hop movements that are huge in Brazil. He was a visionary."[14]

To play a little game of historical what-ifs, consider what might have happened if Tim Maia didn't temporarily ditch his hit-machine in 1974 for the promise of rational immunization? Oberdan Magalhães, Serginho Trombone, Luiz Carlos Batera, and Robson Jorge all jumped ship from Tim's band for more lucrative work during Tim's Rational detour. It's fair to assume that if Tim hadn't changed course so abruptly these guys would have stayed on as well-paid sidemen to one of Brazil's biggest stars. As the most promising and experienced of Tim's bandmates at the outset of Tim's Rational phase, they were the ones most likely and able to find paying work outside of Tim's band. In 1976, the first three went on to found Banda Black

Rio, Brazil's quintessential funk band, something like a Brazilian Earth, Wind & Fire. Robson Jorge teamed up with Lincoln Olivetti in 1976 and spent the next ten years living and working in the studio, writing, playing on, and producing soulful, funky, and modern hits for everyone from Gal Costa and Gilberto Gil to Erasmo Carlos and Xuxa (a sexy children's TV show host) and Jorge Ben Jor.

If you wanted to play soul, funk, or disco music in Brazil, you need to know how to play Tim's music. "Everyone knew his repertoire," Paulinho Trompete #2 (Paulinho Martins) says. Beyond all of the cover bands and small-town band leaders, all of the pros in the scene were connected in some way or another to Tim; they were either on Tim's good side or his bad side. "His band had thirty people. 'Serginho [Trombone] can't play, call Oberdan. If Paulinho Trompete can't play, call the other Paulinho Trompete.'" Paulinho Trompete #1 recalls, "and the one who was always there was Paulinho Guitarra."

Not only did Tim Maia succeed in introducing soul music to Brazil beginning in 1969, by the mid-1970s at the height of his Seroma phase, he pushed Soul Brasileiro beyond a derivative style cleverly mimicking the sound and feel of North American soul sound to a fusion of Brazilian musical traditions with North American soul, funk, and jazz styles. Tim elevated Brazil's contribution to the diasporic soul stew with his unparalleled output between the years 1973 and 1977, the Seroma years, with *Tim Maia Racional* Vol. 1, *Tim Maia Racional* Vol. 2 and *Tim Maia Racional* Vol. 3 being the centerpieces.

If there's one message I feel compelled to leave the reader with, the message repeated again and again to me by almost

Figure 21 *The author with Paulinho Guitarra. June 2016. Photo courtesy of author.*

everyone I interviewed, mostly friends and bandmates of Tim's from these years, is that Tim was really not the guy that the Brazilian media wants you to believe he was. Mostly to blame is the entertaining, but largely fictional 2014 biopic, but more importantly, the consistent sensationalizing of Tim's eccentricities in the Brazilian media. Let's give Tim's old friend and band leader, Paulinho Guitarra, the final words:

> I have to say to you, it was really great. Tim Maia was a great teacher, he was really cool. After I stopped playing with him, I don't know . . . but while I was playing and living with him, he was a very cool person. I was with him every day, all day,

and I learned a lot. . . . Tim Maia's home was always full of lots of musicians: Hyldon, Cassiano, Fábio, Robson Jorge, lots of musicians. Tim Maia was surrounded by musicians all the time. He was very loved by musicians.

Lots of people think lots of things about Tim, but he had a side that was really good, and a side that people loved to talk about in the press. But I always like to talk about the good side of Tim Maia, because his bad side was the same bad side that everybody has, [dealing] with the problems we all have in our lives, it's normal. But the musical part, the part I learned, and I cherish in my memory, there's nothing bad about that. I like to share these good things, because, really, Tim Maia was Brazil's greatest singer.

Notes

Preface

1 Quote taken from Celso Masson, "Fenômeno Racional," *Revista Trip* (Rio de Janeiro, Brazil, October 2001).

2 Linguistic note: I will use the word "Rational" in place of "Racional" except when referring to the actual title of the recordings, such as *Tim Maia Racional* Vol. 1.

3 Seu is an honorific truncation for "Senhor," the same Seu in "Seu Jorge."

4 John Seabrook, "Tarrytown Boy," *The New Yorker* (January 28, 2013) http://www.newyorker.com/magazine/2013/01/28/tarrytown-boy

5 Wax Poetics, issue #36, Summer 2009, the "Brazil Issue."

Introduction

1 Fábio, *Até Parece Que Foi um Sonho*, p. 94.

2 *Rolling Stone* (Brasil) (October 2007) http://rollingstone.uol.com.br/listas/os-100-maiores-discos-da-musica-brasileira/

3 Ben Ratliff, "The Primer: Tropicália and Beyond," *The Wire* (London, June 1999).

4 Nelson Motta, *Vale Tudo*, p. 198.

5 Christopher Dunn, *Brutality Garden*, p. 74.

6   Larry Rohter, "He's Back, Baby: The Man Who Put The Funk In Rio," *New York Times* (October 12, 2012).

7   Rohter, "He's Back, Baby."

8   *Tim Maia* (Polydor, 1970), *Tim Maia* (Polydor, 1971), *Tim Maia* (Polydor, 1972), *Tim Maia* (Polydor, 1973).

9   Author's interview with Paul Heck.

10   *Tim Maia* (Globo Filmes, Rio de Janeiro, Brazil, 2014).

11   Guilherme Genestreti, "Tim Maia' retrata drogas, solidão da fama e tempermento explosivo," *A Folha de São Paulo* (São Paulo, Brazil, October 30, 2014).

12   Christopher Partridge (ed.), *New Religions: A Guide*, p. 10.

13   Author's interview with Tibério Gaspar.

Chapter 1

1   *Marmiteiro*, lunch delivery boy.

2   Erasmo Carlos, *Meu Fama de Mau*, p. 69.

3   Author's interview with Eduardo Araújo.

4   *Malandragem*, a Brazilian term for bohemian lifestyle—an ethos of idleness, fast living, and petty crime—traditionally celebrated in samba lyrics.

5   DVD: *Tim Maia Programa Ensaio* (Unimar Music, 1992).

6   Author's interview with Roger Bruno.

7   The concert took place on November 21, 1962, as described in Ruy Castro, *Bossa Nova*, pp. 243–5.

8   The 1964 coup d'état was a series of events taking place between March 31 and April 1, 1964.

9   Pedro Alexandre Sanches, *Como Dois E Dois São Cinco: Roberto Carlos (& Erasmo & Wanderléa)*, p. 205, which references article from *A Folha de São Paulo* (São Paulo, Brazil, February 24, 1991).

10   Ruy Castro, "Playboy Entrevista: Tim Maia," *Playboy* (Brasil, July 1991).

11   Author's interview with Laercio de Freitas.

12   Author's Interview with Sérgio Dias Baptista (Os Mutantes).

13   André Midani, *Música, Ídolos E Poder*, p. 118.

14   Motta, *Vale Tudo*, pp. 204–5.

15   According to the *Enciclopédia da Música Brasileira* (1998).

16   Motta, *Vale Tudo*, p. 114.

17   Author's interview with Ed Motta.

Chapter 2

1   Within the Candomblé religion, some practitioners are possessed by a specific spirit known as *Preto Velho* (The Old Black Man) who likes to drink booze and smoke cigars. The *cambono* serves as the aid for the *Preto Velho*.

2   Motta, *Vale Tudo*, p. 126.

3   Tim Maia's performance at the 1974 Teatro Bandeirantes Grand Opening: https://www.youtube.com/watch?v=6S8n_EG496I

4   Author's interview with Hyldon da Souza.

5   Motta, *Vale Tudo*, p. 118.

6   Hyldon's rendition translated with help thanks to Bruno Morais.

7   Midani, *Música, Ídolos E Poder*.

8 Original Portuguese: "Alo, Alo, Dom Paulo, Aqui está tudo legal. Estou tratando de levar as caixas Altec. Encontrei todo mundo e foi surpreza geral. Comprei uma Pastor Branco, chama se Claid. Estou levando comigo daqui a pouco estarei ai. Até la, um abraco, Tim Maia."

9 Motta, *Vale Tudo*, p. 101.

10 Ibid., p. 127.

11 Ibid., p. 128.

12 Ibid.

13 Ibid., p. 127.

14 Author's interview with Paulo Roberto de Oliveira (a.k.a. Paulinho Trompete #1).

15 Motta, *Vale Tudo*, p. 128.

Interlude: Seu Manoel and Rational Culture

1 Lewis Carrol, *Through the Looking Glass*, Chapter 5.

2 David V. Barrett, *The New Believers*, p. 384–5.

3 Author's interview with Raphael and Christine of Rational Culture.

4 Initially, Manoel Jacinto Coelho wrote three books that were in print through the early 1970s, then he began expanding upon these teachings across another 977 volumes before his death in 1991. When Tibério and Tim first started reading the books, there were only the first three volumes, distinctive with their yellow covers.

5   https://en.wikipedia.org/wiki/Umbanda

6   Joseph A. Page, *The Brazilians*, pp. 364–6.

7   Stefan Zweig, *Brazil: Land of the Future* (original title: *Brasilien: Ein Land der Zukunft*; Bermann-Fischer, Stockholm [1941]).

8   Ricardo Neumann, "Cultura Racional e Letramento."

9   Neumann, "Cultura Racional e Letramento."

Chapter 3

1   Motta, *Vale Tudo*, p. 127.

2   Ibid.

3   Author's interview with Tibério Gaspar: "He [Manoel Jacintho Coelho] came to me and said: 'Look, you are a person with lots of light, very strong. I wanted to tell you that there are some things that I think will happen in your life. . . . The first song that you make after leaving here [with your partner, Antonio Adolfo] will be a hit in Brazil and will launch you internationally.' That said, the first song I did when I left there was 'Sá Marina,' which made me famous throughout Brazil and was a worldwide hit! And he spoke more: 'Your partner, Antonio Adolfo, you will continue with him until a certain day, then you're going to separate because of a woman.' Actually, this happened because Antonio was best man at my first marriage and I separated with this first wife and he married her. And today, it's okay. For me, there was nothing, because I did not like her, there was absolutely nothing, but that was a little bit of weird business. . . . Then the old black man said the following: 'You will marry three times, but you will only legally marry with the third person and this person will be the love of your life. She will have light eyes and a birthmark the shape of a serpent and she will give you a son that looks like you. You will have only one son with her with eyes the same color as yours.' It happened that I married the first time, took her there and he said, 'This is not the one, you will see.' I spent some time, got separated, then married again and he said, 'This one also will not work.' Then the day I presented Cristina to him, he predicted nothing more."

4   Author's interview with Tibério Gaspar.

5   Tárik de Souza, "Tim Maia—A Volta Do Radical Apóstolo da Competência Musical," *Jornal do Brasil* (June 8, 1982).

6   From a previously unpublished interview from 1995 between Tim Maia and journalists Marcio Gaspar and Lauro Lisboa Garcia: http://hyldon.com.br/entrevista-inedita-com-tim-maia/ : "My interest is fully UFO, transcendental. I have no interest in anything here. I think here we're very confused. . . . I was speaking yesterday with other reporters from another magazine there, there are intraterrestrial beings, man. It's proven, man, the whole world knows it. There are beings that inhabit the center of the earth. . . . We are visited by ninety different beings from different galaxies, different dimensions and there are other things! There are beings of the future, but there's another thing. What I'm saying is a current thing, extraterrestrial beings from other galaxies. And beings that come from our own earth, which inhabit the center of the earth. They are called 'Lunar.' They are white beings because they do not see the sun . . . there are women there who have had sex with strange beings, it's everywhere."

7   Castro, "Playboy Entrevista."

8   Motta, *Vale Tudo*, p. 132.

9   Ibid.

10 Tim Maia's introduction in Portuguese to "Immunização Racional (Que Beleza)" from the August 12, 1974, Bandeirantes Theater Grand Opening: "A proxima música que vamos transar aqui é uma música sobre um livro que eu estou lendo, que eu acho vocês devem ler, chama-se Universo Em Desencanto, e sobre immunização racional."

11 Motta, *Vale Tudo*, p. 136.

12 During Brazil's military dictatorship every song was required to be approved by government censors, forcing lyricists to find ever more clever ways of hiding their social and political critiques within their songs.

13 Motta, *Vale Tudo*, p. 134.

14 Castro, "Playboy Entrevista."

Interlude: Searching for Light during Brazil's Dark Years

1   Cláudio Tsuyoshi Suenaga, "Cultura Racional: O Desencanto Da Seita," www.ufo.com.br/artigos/cultura-racional-o-desencanto-da-seita. Documentary film: *The Source Family* (TriCal Entertainment, USA, 2012).

2   Liner notes from CD reissue: *Tim Maia Racional Vol. 1* (Editora Abril, Brazil, 2011).

3   Motta, *Vale Tudo*, p. 139.

4   Ricardo Neumann, "A Cultura Racional e A Circularidade Cultural." http://www.dhi.uem.br/gtreligiao/pdf/st8/Neumann,%20Ricardo.pdf

5   Neumann, "A Cultura Racional e A Circularidade Cultural."

6   Previously unpublished interview from 1995 between Tim Maia and journalists Marcio Gaspar and Lauro Lisboa Garcia: http://hyldon.com.br/entrevista-inedita-com-tim-maia/

7   "Mundo De Paz E Amor" from *Nossas Raizes* (Alvorado, 1974) and "Alegria Minha Gente" and "A Luz Do Saber" from *Alegria Minha Gente* (Alvorado, 1978).

Chapter 5

1   Motta, *Vale Tudo*, p. 137.

2   Castro, "Playboy Entrevista: Tim Maia."

3   Feature-length docudrama: *Por Toda A Minha Vida* (Globo, Brazil, 2007).

4   Motta, *Vale Tudo*, p. 141.

5   Author's interview with Raphael Racional.

6   Unknown Author, "Tim Maia Agora É Guru," *Revista Pop* (Brazil, January 1975).

7   Motta, *Vale Tudo*, pp. 138–9.

8   Carlos, *Meu Fama De Mau*, p. 231.

9   Greg Casseus, "The Saga of Wilson Simonal," *Wax Poetics Magazine* (New York, NY: Spring, 2004, Issue #8).

10   Sanches, *Como Dois E Dois São Cinco*, p. 209.

11   Ibid., p. 210.

12   Unknown Author, "Tim Maia Agora É Guru."

13   Author's interview with Ed Motta.

Chapter 6

1   Bandeirantes Theater clip link: https://youtu.be/FvIUpxQ3v_g

2   de Souza, "Tim Maia—A Volta Do Radical Apóstolo da Competência Musical."

3   *Sem nota fiscal*, tax free.

4   de Souza, "Tim Maia—A Volta Do Radical Apóstolo da Competência Musical."

Chapter 7

1   In the official release of *Tim Maia Racional* Vol. 3, Don Pi is not given credit, as his parts were re-recorded by Lincoln Olivetti, but his omission from the credits was unlikely accidental.

2   Author's interview with Ed Motta.

Chapter 8

1   Previously unpublished interview from 1995 between Tim Maia and journalists Marcio Gaspar and Lauro Lisboa Garcia: http://hyldon.com.br/entrevista-inedita-com-tim-maia/

2   Castro, "Playboy Entrevista: Tim Maia."

3   WhatsApp message from Raphael Racional.

4   Castro, "Playboy Entrevista: Tim Maia."

5   Ibid.

6   Ibid.

7   Motta, *Vale Tudo*, p. 143.

8   de Souza, "Tim Maia—A Volta Do Radical Apóstolo da Competência Musical."

9   Sitting among the other (now highly collectable) boxes of the *Tim Maia Racional* Vol. 1 and *Tim Maia Racional* Vol. 2 records, Don Pi also stashed a box or two of these unreleased *Tim Maia Racional* singles. "Never been released. I mean, everything was released by Tim Maia's record company, Seroma enterprise or whatever. But this one I didn't throw away. It's at my mother's house. I have to work on it because it's really rotten; it's really white [moldy] like cotton, which happens in humid places like there. But I'm the only one who has this." He acknowledges that other band members possibly received boxes of this record, but if everyone threw them away, as instructed by Tim, Pi's might be the only in existence. So, what's on this lost Tim Maia Racional single? "It's an instrumental recording," Don Pi explains from his faded memory of the recording. "We did some instrumentals with backing vocals and one of the song's is called 'Rio de Janeiro Blue' or something like this and the other one was called 'Topete.' Topete is what I've got here [as he gestures over Skype to the tuft of hair right above the forehead, or forelock]." Pi's description and memory of the record are fairly convincing and while Paulinho Guitarra didn't out right refute Pi's assertion, he does remember them recording a single around this time that was never released.

"I remember we did a single with two songs, one called 'Johnny', it's the original version [a later version appears on *Tim Maia Disco Club* from 1978] that was made after Rational on Seroma. I'm not sure what happened. I remember recording that one and 'Ela Partiu' on the same day in the studio." We know that "Ela Partiu" and "Meus Inimigos" were released as a Seroma single in early 1976 and I made sure Pi wasn't getting confused with the other Rational singles discussed above. At the time of submitting this manuscript, Pi's mother had recently passed away and he'd not yet had a good opportunity to further investigate these boxes in storage at his mother's house.

Chapter 9

1   Barrett, *The New Believers*, pp. 53–4.

2   The album was recorded in 1975, but not pressed and released until a few years later, unofficially distributed locally and through word of mouth. There are no dates on the album, therefore most discographies identify it as being released in 1978.

3   Motta, *Vale Tudo*, p. 146.

4   Unpublished song by song notes written by Don Pi courtesy of Yale Evelev, Luaka Bop.

5   Tim Maia promotional video circa 1976: https://www.youtube.com/watch?v=ewzCP3DYrbc

6   Unpublished song by song notes written by Don Pi courtesy of Yale Evelev, Luaka Bop.

7   Author's interview with Don Pi.

8   de Souza, "Tim Maia—A Volta Do Radical Apóstolo da Competência Musical."

9   Video: My Tracks—Ed Motta: https://www.youtube.com/watch?v=cpNK5H7QmFQ

10   Back cover notes from *Tim Maia* (Som Livre, 1977).

11   Motta, *Vale Tudo*, p. 165.

12   de Souza, "Tim Maia—A Volta Do Radical Apóstolo da Competência Musical."

13   Motta, *Vale Tudo*, p. 212.

14   Ibid., p. 249.

15   Author's interview with Raphael Racional.

Chapter 10

1   Marcelo D2, *Eu Tiro É Onda* (Sony Brazil, 1998).

2   A reference to Chico Recarey, who owned multiple high-profile night clubs in the 1980s and 1990s.

3   Castro, "Playboy Entrevista: Tim Maia."

4   Motta, *Vale Tudo*, p. 312.

5   Pedro Alexandre Sanches, "Gal se equilibria entre 'novos' e 'velhos,'" *A Folha de São Paulo* (São Paulo, Brazil, December 2, 1998).

6   Mano Brown (founding member of Racionais MC's) from: *Racionais MC's—TV Cultura—Ensaio Part 2*: https://www.youtube.com/watch?v=mCV-SliGeyg&feature=youtu.be&t=45

7   Leandro Fortino, "D2 Canta Tim em Noite Underground," *Folha de São Paulo* (June 10, 1998).

8   Carlos Palombini, "Funk Carioca and Música Soul".

Chapter 11

1   Author's interview with Alexandre Kassin.

2   Author's interview with William Luna Jr.

3   Willie Weeks is an in-demand North American studio and live bass player, known for his work with David Bowie, George Harrison, and Donny Hathaway, which is probably the reference Paulinho Guitarra is referring to.

Interlude: Carmelo, Tell Me What to Do

1   Karina Maia and Leandro Souto Maior, "Herança Musical do Filho de Tim Maia é Questionada por Antigos Parceiros," *O Dia Online* (November 4, 2014). http://odia.ig.com.br/diversao/2014-11-04/heranca-musical-do-filho-de-tim-maia-e-questionada-por-antigos-parceiros.html

2   Facebook post on Carlos Cajueiro's wall from October 31, 2014: https://www.facebook.com/photo.php?fbid=779161175476247&set=a.356856551040047.81417.100001471151009&type=3

3   Emmanuel Bonfim, "Criolo E Ivete Sangalo Vão Fazer Turne ao Homenagem a Tim Maia," *A Folha de São Paulo* (São Paulo, Brazil, February 5, 2015).

4 Bonfim, "Criolo E Ivete Sangalo Vão Fazer Turne ao Homenagem a Tim Maia."

Conclusion

1 Donny Hathaway covered the song on his live album but it was originally recorded on his 1971 album, *Imagine.*

2 Castro, "Playboy Entrevista: Tim Maia."

3 Ibid.

4 Author's interview with Antonio Adolfo.

5 Jamari França, "Tim Maia – Mistura Rock, Xaxado, Samba, Jazz, Soul e Outros Sons no Circo Voador," *Jornal do Brasil* (March 4, 1983).

6 *Samba de Breque* is a subgenre of samba characterized by sudden pauses in the syncopated rhythm of the music. The silence is filled by declamatory speeches from the singer, usually in a satirical manner. From: https://pt.wikipedia.org/wiki/Samba_de_breque.

7 Jamari França, "Tim Maia – Mistura Rock, Xaxado, Samba, Jazz, Soul e Outros Sons no Circo Voador."

8 Author's interview with Laercio de Freitas and Thalma de Freitas.

9 de Souza, "Tim Maia – A Volta Do Radical Apóstolo da Competência Musical."

10 Veja interview with Eduardo Araújo by Sergio Martins: http://www.rockbrasileiro.net/2016/09/eduardo-araujo-ele-ainda-e-o-bom-no.html

11   Author interview with Rodrigo Piza.

12   França, "Tim Maia – Mistura Rock, Xaxado, Samba, Jazz, Soul e
      Outros Sons no Circo Voador."

13   Ibid.

14   Author interview with Béco Dranoff.

List of Interviews

Paulo Ricardo Alves a.k.a. Paulinho Guitarra in Portuguese, June 14, 2016 (Niterói, Brazil)

Reginaldo Francisco a.k.a. Dom Pi in English, April 24 and October 17, 2016 (Skype)

Tibério Gaspar in Portuguese, June 15 and 16, 2016 (Rio de Janeiro and Paquetá, Brazil)

Sergio Martins in English, January 21, February 17 and June 10, 2016 (Skype and Rio de Janeiro, Brazil)

Paulo Roberto de Oliveira a.k.a. Paulinho Trompete #1 in Portuguese, January 12, 2016 (Skype)

Paulinho Martins a.k.a. Paulinho Trompete #2 in Portuguese, January 16, 2016 (Rio de Janeiro, Brazil)

Hyldon De Souza in Portuguese, June 14, 2016 (Rio de Janeiro, Brazil)

Kassin Kamal in English, June 15, 2016 (Rio de Janeiro, Brazil)

Ed Motta in English, February 11, 2016 (Skype)

Antonio Adolfo in English, July 20, 2017 (Skype)

Sérgio Dias Baptista (Os Mutantes) in English, July 17, 2007 (New York, NY)

Eduardo Araújo in Portuguese, June 10, 2016 (São Paulo, Brazil)

Laercio de Freitas and Thalma de Freitas in Portuguese and English, February 24, 2017 (San Diego, CA)

Raphael and Christine Racional in Portuguese (two current members/practitioners of Rational Culture who preferred to not give their unrelated family names), June 14, 2016 (Rio de Janeiro, Brazil)

Rodrigo Piza in Portuguese, August 28, 2016 (email)
Yale Evelev in English, July 19, 2016 (New York, NY)
Béco Dranoff in English, September 23, 2016 (email)
Paul Heck in English, May 17, 2016 (telephone)
David Galasse in English, November 8, 2016 (email)
Roger Bruno in English, November 29, 2007 (Tarrytown, NY)

Works Cited

Barrett, David V., *The New Believers* (London: Cassel & Co., 2001).

Carlos, Erasmo, *Meu Fama De Mau* (Rio de Janeiro, Brasil: Objetiva, 2007).

Castro, Ruy, "Playboy Entrevista: Tim Maia," *Playboy* (Brasil, July 1991).

Castro, Ruy, *Bossa Nova – The Story of the Brazilian Music That Seduced the World* (Chicago: A Cappella, 2000).

De Souza, Tárik, "Tim Maia – A Volta Do Radical Apóstolo da Competência Musical," *Jornal do Brasil* (June 8, 1982).

Dunn, Christopher, *Brutality Garden: Tropicália and the Emergence of a Brazilian Counterculture* (Chapel Hill: University of North Carolina Press, 2001).

Fábio as told to Achel Tinoco, *Até Parece Que Foi Sonho* (Brazil: Matrix, 2007).

França, Jamari, "Tim Maia – Mistura Rock, Xaxado, Samba, Jazz, Soul e Outros Sons no Circo Voador," *Jornal do Brasil* (March 4, 1983).

Genestreti, Guilherme, "Tim Maia' retrata drogas, solidão da fama e tempermento explosive," *Folha de São Paulo* (São Paulo, Brazil, October 30, 2014).

Liner notes from Tim Maia Racional Vol. 1, 2 & 3 (Editora Abril, 2011).

Martins, Sergio, "Eduardo Araújo: Ele ainda é O Bom," *Veja Música Online* (São Paulo, Brazil, September 25, 2016).

Midani, André, *Música, Ídolos E Poder* (Brazil: Editora Nova Fronteira, 2008).

Motta, Nelson, *Noites Tropicais* (Rio de Janeiro Objetiva, 2000).

Motta, Nelson, *Vale Tudo: O Som e a Fúria de Tim Maia* (Brazil: Objetiva, 2007).

Neumann, Ricardo, "Cultura Racional e Letramento," *ANPUH – XXIV Simpósio Nacional de História – São Leopoldo*, 2007, https://anais. anpuh.org/?p=15455

Page, Joseph A., *The Brazilians* (New York: Perseus Books, 1995).

Palombini, Carlos, "Funk Carioca and Música Soul," in John Shepherd and John Heard (eds.), *Bloomsbury Encyclopedia of Popular Music of the World: Volume IX: Genres: Caribbean and Latin America* (London and New York: Bloomsbury, 2014).

Partridge, Christopher (ed.), *New Religions: A Guide* (Oxford, UK: Oneworld, 2004).

Por Toda A Minha Vida [Feature-length Docu-Drama] (Brazil: Globo, 2007).

Previously unpublished interview from 1995 between Tim Maia and journalists Marcio Gaspar and Lauro Lisboa Garcia: http:// hyldon.com.br/entrevista-inedita-com-tim-maia/

Rohter, Larry, "He's Back, Baby: The Man Who Put The Funk In Rio," *New York Times* (New York, October 12, 2012).

Sanches, Pedro Alexandre, *Como Dois E Dois São Cinco: Roberto Carlos (& Erasmo & Wanderléa)* (São Paulo, Brazil: Boitempo Editorial, 2004).

"Tim Maia Agora É Guru," *Revista Pop* (Brazil, January 1975).

Index